The

Senior's Guide
to Easy Computing
with Vista
Basics, Internet, and E-Mail

The
Senior's Guide
to Easy Computing
with Vista

Basics, Internet, and E-Mail

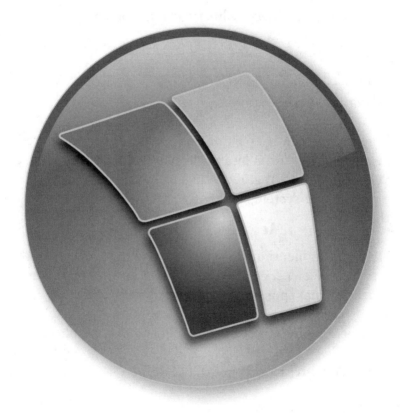

By Rebecca Sharp Colmer and Flip Colmer
EKLEKTIKA PRESS
Chelsea, Michigan

Table of Contents

Table of Contents

Table of Contents

Table of Contents

Table of Contents

Table of Contents

Table of Contents

Disclaimer

Every effort has been made to make this book as complete as possible and as accurate as possible. However, there may be mistakes both typographical and in content. Therefore, this text should be used as a general guide and not the ultimate source of information.

LIMIT OF LIABILITY/DISCLAIMER OF WARRANTY: THE PUBLISHER AND THE AUTHORS MAKE NO REPRESENTATIONS OR WARRANTIES WITH RESPECT TO THE ACCURACY OR COMPLETENESS OF THE CONTENTS OF THIS WORK AND SPECIFICALLY DISCLAIM ALL WARRANTIES, INCLUDING WITHOUT LIMITATION WARRANTIES OF FITNESS FOR A PARTICULAR PURPOSE. NO WARRANTY MAY BE CREATED OR EXTENDED BY SALES OR PROMOTIONAL MATERIALS. THE ADVICE AND STRATEGIES CONTAINED HEREIN MAY NOT BE SUITABLE FOR EVERY SITUATION. THIS WORK IS SOLD WITH THE UNDERSTANDING THAT THE PUBLISHER IS NOT ENGAGED IN RENDERING LEGAL, ACCOUNTING, OR OTHER PROFESSIONAL SERVICES. IF PROFESSIONAL ASSISTANCE IS REQUIRED, THE SERVICES OF A COMPETENT PROFESSIONAL PERSON SHOULD BE SOUGHT. NEITHER THE PUBLISHER NOR THE AUTHORS SHALL BE LIABLE FOR DAMAGES ARISING HEREFROM. THE FACT THAT AN ORGANIZATION OR WEB SITE IS REFERRED TO IN THIS WORK AS A CITATION AND/OR POTENTIAL SOURCE OF FURTHER INFORMATION DOES NOT MEAN THAT THE AUTHORS OR THE PUBLISHER ENDORSES THE INFORMATION THE ORGANIZATION OR WEB SITE MAY PROVIDE OR RECOMMENDATIONS IT MAY MAKE. FURTHER, READERS SHOULD BE AWARE THAT INTERNET WEB SITES LISTED IN THIS WORK MAY HAVE CHANGED OR DISAPPEARED BETWEEN WHEN IT WAS WRITTEN AND WHEN IT IS READ. NEITHER THE PUBLISHER NOR AUTHORS SHALL BE LIABLE FOR ANY LOSS OF PROFIT OR ANY OTHER COMMERCIAL DAMAGES, INCLUDING BUT NOT LIMITED TO SPECIAL, INCIDENTAL, CONSEQUENTIAL, OR OTHER DAMAGES. THE AUTHORS AND PUBLISHER SPECIFICALLY DISCLAIM ANY LIABILITY, LOSS, OR RISK, PERSONAL OR OTHERWISE, WHICH IS INCURRED AS A CONSEQUENCE, DIRECTLY OR INDIRECTLY, OF THE USE AND APPLICATION OF ANY OF THE CONTENTS OF THIS BOOK.

Getting The Most From This Book

This is a book that assumes you have little to no experience with computers.

It is best to sit down in front of a computer as you read this book. That way you can do, or see, what we are describing in the book. Follow the steps we tell you and you will see things happen on the screen.

Like most new skills, practice makes perfect. If you are new to computers, you will need to learn and practice new skills.

If you are upgrading from a previous version of Windows, you will need to change some habits that you have established. Not everything has changed with Vista, but it will take some practice to get familiar with the changes that have been made.

Objectives And Limitations

Let us make one thing clear right at the beginning. This book is not a textbook on how to learn everything there is to know about computers.

Rather, it is an organized collection of PC, Internet, and e-mail fundamentals.

This is a crash course in "basics." It's simple. It's fun. It will get you going fast!

This book will help you to become computer functional, but not necessarily computer literate. We'll leave the techno-babble to the "propeller heads." We're going to give you some basics so you can make good use of your computer starting today!

Assumptions

One assumption we made as we wrote this book is that you have a broadband Internet connection. That means you connect to the Internet via a cable modem, a DSL line or a satellite dish. It also means that you can go out on the Internet by just clicking your e-mail client or browser.

If you have a dialup connection, in other words, you use your telephone line to access the Internet, you will need to connect to the Internet first, before you accomplish any of the tasks that reference the Internet.

Unless otherwise stated, when we talk about a browser we are referring to Microsoft's Internet Explorer. When we talk about an e-mail client, we are referring to Microsoft's Windows Mail.

Are you scratching your head because all of this makes no sense? Don't worry; we cover all of these things in more detail later in the book.

We Want To Hear From You!

Send us an e-mail about your computing stories. Feel free to e-mail us your questions. We'll be glad to help if we can. If you have a question, please include the following information:

- Type of computer and operating system you are using.
- Internet Service Provider and type of connection.
- What you are trying to do and which program you are using.

Our Web site: www.theseniorsguide.com

You can always contact us the old-fashioned way:

The Senior's Guide Series
EKLEKTIKA Press
P.O. Box 157
Chelsea, MI 48118

PART 1

Understanding PC Basics

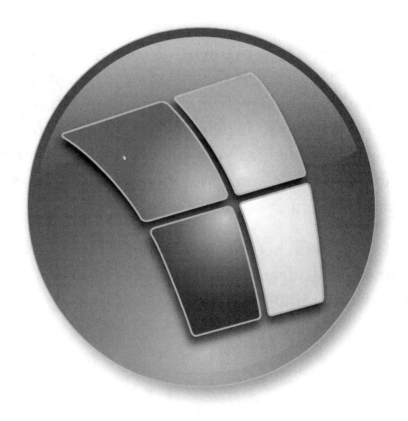

What Is A Personal Computer (PC)?

A personal computer (PC) is a stand-alone computer that is equipped with a central processing unit (CPU), one or more disk drives, random access memory (RAM), a monitor, a keyboard, and a mouse.

It comes in an assortment of colors, shapes and sizes. A PC is a device that allows you to communicate with businesses, friends, family and strangers around the world. It helps to organize all of your information such as your personal address book, your checkbook, and your photos if you have a digital camera or scanner.

Your PC will become a teacher of new skills, games, and ideas. Your computer is YOUR personal assistant.

Is A Mac (Apple Macintosh) A PC?

No! In 1981 IBM introduced a personal computer called the IBM PC. Other manufacturers created computers that work just like the IBM model and they are all called PCs as well.

Although the Apple Macintosh (Mac) is small and personal, it uses a different operating system and is not called a PC.

Think of it as the difference between an audio CD and a DVD. The result is the same: beautiful music or video, playing for your enjoyment. However, CDs and DVDs are not totally interchangeable.

Macs now have the ability to run most PC software. PCs on the other hand cannot run Mac software.

What Is Hardware?

Hardware is a term for the physical components that are included when you purchase a PC. They include the system box, monitor, keyboard and mouse.

You can purchase additional hardware items such as modems, CD-ROM drives, DVD drives, video and digital cameras and whatever else the "propeller heads" invent. As your needs grow, your computer can as well.

By itself, hardware is not capable of doing anything. Look at your stereo. It sits there looking nice, without emitting sounds until the hardware pieces are given the sounds to play.

Just like the stereo, your computer needs something to make it work. That something is called software.

What Is Software?

Software tells the hardware how to work, what to do, and when to do it.

Software is what gives your computer its identity. It includes the basic operating system, utility and application programs, all expressed in a language your hardware understands.

Think about when you first balanced your checkbook. Either someone showed you how to do it or you followed the instructions on the back of the statement. Those instructions "programmed" you on how to do the task at hand: balancing your checkbook.

Those instructions were your "software" and you were the "hardware" that did the work.

There is software to tell your computer to do just about any task you want or can think of.

What Are Applications?

Software applications are programs that a computer uses so that it can accomplish predetermined tasks.

Each application performs a specific kind of work, such as, word processing, desktop publishing, accounting, music downloading, personal finance, etc.

There is an application for just about any task you can think of. Do you want to organize your stamp collection? There's software to help you do just that. Do you want to design your next home? Yes, software exists for that, too.

A utility program is an after-market application that does housekeeping operations to assist you in maintaining and improving your computer's performance.

What Is An Operating System/CPU?

An operating system (Vista) is the master control program for the computer. It is the stored information that your computer needs to operate. Without an operating system, all of the hardware would just sit there and collect dust!

The CPU (central processing unit) is the computer chip that does all of the processing for the computer. Inside this tiny chip are millions of transistors (electrical switches) that carry out mathematical calculations. Everything a computer does is essentially a mathematical equation.

We measure the CPU's speed (its ability to do work) in megahertz (MHz) and gigahertz (GHz). GHz is faster than MHz and in the computer world, faster is better. Each year, computers ship from the factory with faster and faster CPU speeds.

What Is RAM?

RAM is the computer's primary working memory.

RAM is used for short-term storage while the computer does its work. It is read/write memory.

The more RAM you have the more your computer can do at one time.

RAM is volatile memory. The computer needs to be running so that RAM "remembers" what it is doing. In case of a system failure or power interruption, you will lose all of your work in RAM that you have not saved on a disk drive. Save your work frequently.

RAM is distinguished from ROM, which is read-only memory. ROM is long-term storage memory and retains the data when the computer is shut down.

What Is The Hard Drive?

The hard drive, or hard disk, is your PC's main storage device. It's sometimes called the C:/ drive and pronounced "see" drive. Data files and programs are magnetically stored there. A typical hard drive holds 80 gigabytes of storage or more.

If you are planning on storing a lot of music or photos on your computer, plan on getting as big a hard drive as your budget will allow. It is very easy to fill a hard drive with entertainment files.

Most computer users only have one hard drive. However, if you need more storage, adding additional hard drives is easy.

What Is The Difference Between RAM And Hard Drive Storage?

Storage is where a program is kept. However, RAM is where it works.

The amount of space a program needs for storage on the hard drive has nothing to do with how much RAM is needed to run the program. Many PC programs take up many megabytes of storage space. Many programs also require at least 128MB of RAM or more, to operate efficiently.

To run today's popular programs make sure your computer has adequate RAM and storage.

If you're buying a new computer, it should have more than enough RAM already installed. Vista needs lots of RAM. We recommend at least 1GB of RAM to run Vista.

If you are getting a "hand me up" from your kids, it may not have enough RAM to run today's newer, larger programs. Check the computer's RAM number to see if it is adequate for your needs.

What Is A Gigabyte?

A gigabyte is a large unit of measurement of storage capacity. Here is how storage capacity is calculated:

- One Bit = smallest amount of info.
- One Byte = eight bits strung together.
- One Kilobyte (KB) or K = 1000 bytes.
- One Megabyte (MB) or meg = about a million bytes.
- One Gigabyte (GB) or gig = about a billion bytes.

All measurements for storage devices are now in gigabytes. Soon, terabytes (1000GB) will be the talk of the town.

To see how much storage you have, simply click on your Computer icon. At the bottom of the new window will be a graph showing how much you have, and how much you've used.

What Are Disk Drives?

Disk drives allow you to store and move data from and to different types of media.

There are several types of drives: floppy drive, hard drive, CD drive, DVD drive, external hard drive, removable drive and portable drive. Floppy drives are almost obsolete as they cannot hold much data.

Because the computer world is ever-changing, expect to see new drives in the future that will run our programs faster and make our tasks much simpler. In the computer world, change is good. However, you do not have to change computers every time a "new" improvement is made.

The biggest difference in drives is size or capacity. Drives also differ in how fast they take to find and access information.

What Is A CD Drive?

CDs are compact discs. They are a removable-storage media unlike the hard drive which stays in the computer. CD drives read the data encoded on the disc and then transfer this data to the computer.

There are two "flavors" of CD drives:

- CD-ROM, which you can read CDs but not record to them.
- CD-RW, which is a re-writeable CD-ROM drive. It allows you to read, erase, and use a rewriteable disc repeatedly.

Not all CD discs are re-writeable. Some are re-writeable multiple times, some only once and some not at all. Read the label and buy the correct discs.

One advantage of CD-RW drives is that you can make audio CDs to use in your car or home stereo. However, sometimes audio CDs you create on your computer may not function in a stereo system's CD player. Don't worry, it wasn't you. Sometimes newer computer CD formats are not compatible with older CD players.

What Is A DVD?

DVD stands for digital versatile disc.

DVD drives read DVDs.

A DVD holds about five gigabytes of information while a CD only holds about 700 megabytes.

A CD drive cannot read a DVD. However, DVD drives can read a CD.

Yes, there are DVD-RW drives and discs for multiple uses. Again, make sure to read the box.

And once again, sometimes DVDs you'll make on your computer may not play in older DVD players attached to TVs.

What Is A Monitor?

Sometimes we call the monitor a CRT (cathode ray tube), video display unit or a LCD (Liquid Crystal Display).

The monitor attaches to the video output of the computer and produces a visual display.

Most computers these days come with a 15-inch flat panel monitor. For an additional cost you can upgrade to a larger monitor. Large monitors are a dream to work with and make it much easier to view your work. Larger flat panel displays take up very little extra room on your desk.

CRT monitors are less expensive than flat panel displays, but take up more desk room — especially if you opt for a larger monitor.

What Is A QWERTY Keyboard?

The QWERTY keyboard is the standard keyboard layout used for computer keyboards.

It is the most frequently used input device for all computers.

The keyboard provides a set of alphabetic, numeric, punctuation, symbol, and control keys.

There are a number of different styles of keyboards you can choose: from basic QWERTY layout to those with many more buttons and functions. You can get wired or wireless keyboards. You can get an ergonomic keyboard that is bent in the middle to give your wrists a rest and prevent repetitive stress injuries. However, it is more expensive than a regular keyboard.

Standard QWERTY Keyboard

What Is A Mouse?

The mouse is a control device. It controls the pointer on your computer screen.

It is housed in a palm-sized case. When you move the mouse on your desk, a corresponding arrow commonly known as "the pointer" moves on the computer screen.

Think of it as a remote control for your computer. Move the mouse left and right, the pointer moves left and right. Move the mouse forward and backward, the pointer moves up and down the screen. Using the mouse to command the computer to do most tasks eliminates many keyboard strokes.

Just like with keyboards, there are many choices as to what mouse you can use. There are big mice, little mice, mice with two buttons and some with more. You can purchase a wireless mouse and make your workspace less cluttered. You can buy packages where you get a wireless mouse and keyboard made by the same company that work well together.

On laptops, there can be other styles of pointing devices: touch pads or control sticks. They perform the same functions as the mouse.

What Are The Mouse Functions?

Pointing. To point to something on the screen, move the mouse across the mouse pad until the pointer is in the spot where you want it. The pointer will move in the same direction that you move the mouse.

Clicking. One mouse click (or one click) is one quick press of the left button of the mouse. Do not hold the button down.

Right Clicking. When you see 'right-click', that means one quick press of the right button of the mouse. Again, do not hold the mouse button down.

Double-clicking. Point and quickly click the left mouse button in rapid succession twice. Double-clicking is also used to initiate action.

Selecting. To select text or an image, place the mouse pointer where you want to start the selection, press and hold down the left mouse button, and then drag the mouse to the ending spot. When you have completed the drag, release the mouse button. Your selection will now be highlighted. Dragging allows you to select text (generally for copying, cutting or removing), to move items, and to perform other tasks.

What Are The Mouse Functions?, Cont.

Scrolling. Some mice have a wheel between the two buttons. This allows you to move up and down a page. In addition, some advanced mice allow you to pivot the wheel left and right to move left and right across a page.

Basic Corded Mouse

Wireless Mouse

What Is The Cursor?

The flashing bar, known as the cursor, is where the work will take place on the computer screen. To move the cursor with the mouse, place the pointer where you want the cursor to appear and click the mouse.

When you start to type, or make inputs via the mouse, it will appear where the cursor is flashing.

I have just made the decision to write a Vista version of my book. It won't be out until next year, but it will be helpful to Vista users. In fact, your letter convinced me it was time to start on this project.

The Cursor Ready to do Work

What Are USB Ports?

USB (Universal Serial Bus) ports are the most common way of connecting devices to a computer. They allow true plug and play capability. If you get a new device, such as a digital camera that is USB, in all likelihood, you will have little to do to set it up for use. Simply plug in the USB cable and Vista does all the rest for your setup.

USB Port and Plug

What Is Multimedia?

Multimedia is a term used to describe any program that incorporates some combination of sound, music, written text, pictures, animation, and video. In fact, the term multimedia is no longer meaningful as all computers generally ship with these abilities. The difference is whether or not a computer has enough computing power to run a really sophisticated, graphics intense game, or if it is just a good DVD or download video platform.

Examples:

- DVD movie
- Downloaded movies, music
- Podcasts
- Interactive Games

What Is A Modem?

A modem is the communications hardware that allows your computer to send and receive information from other computers, over a telephone line, cable TV line or satellite dish.

Most new computers come with internal telephone modems. You will need special modems for DSL, cable or satellite communication devices, usually supplied by the service provider.

You will need a modem (and a telephone line, cable line, or satellite dish) to hook up to online services and the Internet.

If you use a satellite dish, cable TV or a DSL line to connect to the Internet, the modem you will use will most likely be external to the computer and connect to it with cables.

Is Modem Speed Important?

Yes! Common speeds for today's telephone modems are between 28,800 and 56,600 kilobytes per second (expressed as 28.8K and 56.6K). The existing telephone lines and equipment can only handle up to about 56K.

Baud rate is the number of times a modem's signal changes per second when transmitting data. It is how modem speed is measured. The bigger the number, the faster you can communicate.

DSL, cable and satellite modems all have speeds in excess of 56.6K. High-speed modems allow you to download items from the Internet much faster. It is worth it to spend a little extra to get this faster speed.

Is Modem Speed Important?, Cont.

Connection	Speed (Kbps)	Comment
Dial-up	28.8 to 56 **Fair**	Requires a modem and a standard telephone line
ISDN	64 to 128 **OK**	Requires an ISDN modem and an ISDN telephone line
Satellite	400 **Better**	Requires a special modem and outside antenna
Asynchronous Digital Subscriber Line (DSL)	512 to 1,500 **Best**	Requires a special modem and standard telephone line
Cable Modem	512 to 1,500 **Best**	Requires a cable modem and cable service

What Does Wireless Mean?

It used to be that everything on the computer was connected by wires, just like telephones. And just like telephones, many computer components have gone wireless. They connect to the computer via radio signal. This allows you to reduce the number of wires coming out of your computer and declutter your desk.

PART 2

Getting Set Up

How Do I Get Started?

First, you need a computer or at least access to one. You can get access to computers at libraries, schools, recreation centers, cyber-cafes and senior centers, just to name a few places. Now is also a good time to pester your kids or grandkids, or your friends' kids or grandkids, so you can use their computers in the comforts of a home.

Our best advice is not to spend a lot of money on your first computer. Until you have a real good reason to have all the bells and whistles, stick with a basic computer, but one that won't be obsolete in a matter of months.

Windows Vista comes in seven different flavors from stripped down Vista Home Basic to Vista Ultimate. We use Ultimate as we need to be able to answer questions about all the platforms and features. Most everyone would be fine with Vista Home Premium Edition. However, stay away from Vista Home Basic. It just isn't a good version for most folks.

What Is The Best Workspace?

You will need a flat surface with a nearby power source and telephone, cable, or satellite jack. The area should be well lit. Invest in a surge protector. You can plug all the components into the power strip while protecting against power surges.

If you don't have a computer desk (with a keyboard shelf at a good height for typing), be sure you can type comfortably on your keyboard. Your wrists should be flat as you type. If you have to bend your wrists to type you could develop a repetitive stress injury. Be sure that you can view the monitor comfortably. Is it too close or too far? Is it at eye level? Is there any glare?

Once you have picked the best workspace, you can unpack your PC. Remember to save the boxes just in case you ever have to ship your computer.

Keep the manuals and documentation handy.

Your computer will come with a complete set of instructions on how to set it up. It will tell you what cables need connecting, and to where. Most manufacturers have even color-coded the connections. For example, red to red and green to green.

There will be a written "quickstart" guide for you

to read, even though the detailed instructions about the computer are found in the Help menu on the computer. Here are the basic connections you need to make:

- Connect the video cable from the monitor to the monitor connector on the back of the PC.
- Connect the keyboard cable to the keyboard connector on the back of the PC.
- Connect the mouse cable to the mouse connector on the back of the PC.
- Connect the printer to the printer port on the back of the PC. If you have a serial printer, you connect to one of the serial ports. If you have a USB printer, it connects to any of the USB ports.
- Connect the power cord for the monitor to the back of the monitor. The other end will plug into the power source.
- Connect the power cord for the PC to the back of the PC. The other end will plug into the power source.

Be sure to follow the instructions on when to turn on the computer and when to turn on the monitor. There can be a specific order for this for the first start up.

How Do I Turn On The PC?

After you make all of the connections and plug in the power cord, turn on the power switches or buttons. Generally, both the system box and monitor have a power switch.

The power button on the system box is typically located on the front of the machine. You should see an indicator light go on to let you know the machine is on.

The power switch for the monitor is usually located on the front panel. There will be other adjustment buttons on your monitor to fine-tune the picture, just like on your TV. However, for the most part, you will not have to make any adjustments.

If you are using a surge protector, follow closely the instructions in your operations manual.

Remember to follow the manufacturer's instructions on how to set up your computer. If our steps do not coincide with the manufacturer's, follow the manufacturer's instructions.

How Do I Turn Off The PC?

Always follow the prescribed shut down procedures for your computer. You should not just turn it off. You should wait until the software is ready to turn off. Once it is turned off, you can use your surge protector master switch.

Before you shut down, always save the files you are working on. Always close open windows before shutting down your computer. This will help to protect your files from data corruption. To shut down:

- Click the Start button.
- Select the arrow in the lower right corner of the Start Menu.
- Select Shut Down.

It is not the end of the world if you shut down improperly. You may get some extra messages cautioning you not to do that again.

There will be times when your computer will crash or freeze-up for no apparent reason. DON'T PANIC! It is the nature of computers to get confused every once in awhile. It's not your fault! The good news is that Vista is a very stable operating system. It will not freeze-up as often as older versions of Windows.

PART 3

Understanding Windows

What Is The Windows Operating System?

Microsoft Windows (Windows, for short) is the name of the operating system that lets you give orders to your computer.

Vista is the newest version of the Windows operating systems. It offers more tools, buzzers, bells and advantages than older versions. In the future, expect newer versions to come out. However, you do not have to run out and get the newest version every time one is released.

There are different versions of Vista for business and home use. Most home users do not need a full-fledged business version of Vista.

There are compatibility issues between Vista and older hardware and software. You may have to buy new peripherals and upgrade your software when you get a Vista machine. If you're just starting out, it won't be a problem for you as everything will be new.

How Can I Check To See If I Can Upgrade My Existing Computer To Vista?

The Upgrade Advisor is a Microsoft downloadable program that will scan your computer and give you a report on compatibility issues for both the system and your devices. It will also recommend solutions to these conflicts and recommend which version of Vista you should choose.

To start this process,

Go to www.microsoft.com/windowsvista.

- Click on Get Ready.
- Click Windows Vista Upgrade Adviser.
- Download the Installer Package.
- Install the package and then run the scan.

The link to the Upgrade Advisor is at the bottom of the web page, in the middle.

What Is The Desktop?

The Desktop is the working area (background) of the Windows display on your computer.

Look at your desk at home or work. It is the area where you do your paperwork. You pull a file, letter, or checkbook from a drawer, do some work, and put it back when you are finished. The Desktop of a computer is where you will pull out your electronic files, write electronic letters or work in your computer-based checkbook.

When you start your computer, you will see several screens go by before you arrive at the main Windows screen, which is the Desktop.

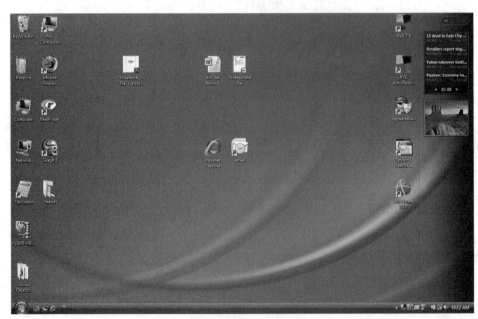

The Desktop

Is It Possible To Customize The Desktop Layout?

Yes! That's what's great about Vista. You can change the appearance to suit your desires. You can move icons around, remove icons, add icons, change the colors and so much more.

If you don't like the standard color scheme on your Desktop, you can change it. You can use pre-defined color schemes or make up your own. If your color selections are too wild they may cause eye strain!

Right-click on an empty portion of the desktop. A pop-up menu appears. Click on Personalize and you will be given a number of tabs to make changes.

Some folks worry that they'll make a change that "ruins" their computer. Don't worry. Play around a bit. You can always put things back the way they were.

What Is The Taskbar?

The Taskbar is the horizontal bar along the bottom of the Desktop. It has the Start Button on the left. Next to the Start button are the Quick Launch icons. Displayed in small rectangles near the middle of the Taskbar are the programs that are running. Near the right side, you will see the programs or tasks that start automatically when you start Windows. On the far right, you will see the time displayed.

The Taskbar allows you to start your navigation process through all of the computer files.

If you would like to move the Taskbar to another location, just move your cursor to the Taskbar, click and hold down the mouse button, and drag the Taskbar to another of the monitor's edges.

To make other adjustments to how the Taskbar works, right-click on the Taskbar and then select Properties from the dialog box. You can make a lot of changes to how the Taskbar works. In fact, for many facets of computing, a right click will bring up dialog boxes that will have properties that you can adjust to enhance your computing experience.

What Is An Icon?

An Icon is a little picture that represents a program, command or a file.

For instance, the Computer Icon looks like a small computer.

Icons that have a small arrow in the lower left corner are called Shortcuts. The arrow indicates that the icon is a shortcut that points to a program, folder, or other item. A shortcut is a quick way to open a program or file.

Since the Shortcut is simply a pointer to a specific program or file, you can delete the shortcut or remove it from the Desktop without actually deleting the program or file.

Icons on the Desktop

What Is The Windows Sidebar And What Are Gadgets?

The Windows Sidebar is a vertical pane that holds small applications that you use frequently. These mini-apps are called Gadgets.

There are hundreds of Gadgets available for your use from calculators to day/night clocks. Want your favorite news feed displayed? You can display that too.

To add a Gadget, click the Down Arrow at the top of the Sidebar. Click Add Gadgets. A list will pop up of all of the available Gadgets. Select the ones that you want. After you install a Gadget, you can customize each one to make them work better for you. You can move the Sidebar to a different loca-

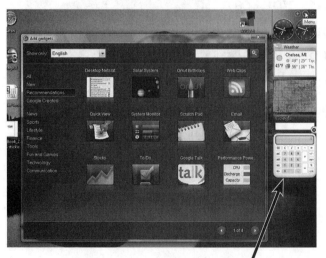

tion or even hide it when you do not want to see it. Right-click at the top of the Sidebar for your choices.

Windows Sidebar with Add Gadgets Dialog Box

What Is The Pointer?

The Pointer is the arrow you use to choose things on screen.

By pointing to a spot in a document, and left clicking, you put the cursor at that location. Now you can do some work there. You can type more text or you can select text for editing. Once text is selected, you can delete, cut, copy or move the selected text.

> By pointing to a spot in a document, and left clicking, you put the cursor at that location. Now you can do some work there I ←

The Pointer Becomes an "I" Bar in a Text Document

You also use the Pointer to select commands from Drop Down Menus, select icon commands from toolbars and navigate around your computer.

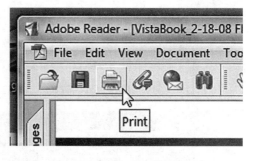

If you would like to change how the pointer looks, right click in a blank area of the desktop. Select Personalize from the dialog box, then select Mouse Pointer. You can choose from many different styles of pointers and can control how the mouse behaves.

How Do I Tell The Difference Between The Disk Drives?

All drives that are attached to a computer are assigned a letter. It's a simple way to tell them apart. The designations are A:, B:, C:, D:, E:, F: etc. As you add more peripheral drives, your computer will automatically assign them a letter.

In the past, the A: drive was for the floppy drive. The B: drive was for a second floppy. The C: drive was the computer's main hard drive. Even though your computer may not have any floppies, by convention, most computers' hard drives are the C: drive. If your computer came with a second installed hard drive, or partitioned your only hard drive into two parts, the second hard drive or part will be the D: drive.

You can see all the drives connected to your computer by clicking on the Computer icon.

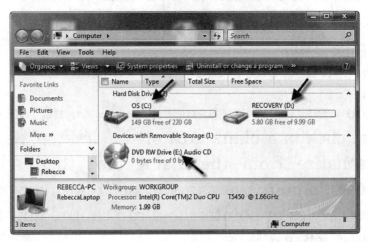

What Is A File?

A File is a collection of information, with a unique name, stored in your computer or on a removable disk.

Your checking account could be one file. A single piece of correspondence could be another file. A collection of correspondence could be in one file. However, as you would in a traditional filing cabinet, a number of different letters (file) might go into a common folder (big file). Some examples:

- A letter to your mother might be Lettertomom.doc
- Your computer-based checkbook might be Mycheckbook.qdf
- And a business spreadsheet might be Balancemybooks.xls

What are those last three letters after the period all about? Just turn the page to find out.

What Is A File Extension?

The last three letters (suffix) of a file name are called an extension.

Every file has a specific format (program that the file was created with). There are many different formats. By naming a file with an extension, you tell the computer the format of the file. That way the computer knows what format to use each time you want to work with that file. The computer will automatically start the correct program. Most programs automatically add the extension suffix when you save your work.

By default, Vista hides all of the file extensions. To make your computer life easier, you should show all of the file extensions, all the time. To show the extensions, click Organize in any folder. Then click Folder and Search Options, then View. Make sure the box labeled Hide Extensions For Known Files Types is unchecked.

What Is A Folder?

Folders allow you to organize information. Just like that file cabinet we mentioned earlier, you should organize all your files into folders. Folders can hold both files and other folders (known as subfolders).

For example, you could put all of your letters to Aunt Mary, in a folder with her name on it. And you could put the Aunt Mary folder into a folder named General Correspondence that holds many other files and folders. Organize your computer as you see fit. But you should organize it right from the beginning.

You can name Folders anything you want. When you create a new folder, you get to name it. Later on, if you need to, you can rename it. And if you ever find you don't need the folder anymore, you can delete it entirely.

Windows Review

- It's your computer so customize it to your needs.
- Use Gadgets to make your Desktop more useful.
- If you use your computer daily, you will become a pro in no time: practice makes perfect.
- Create a logical filing system that you can use at all times.
- Don't be afraid to look around and see what's behind an icon. You really cannot "hurt" the computer.
- Right-clicking brings up alternate menus that allow you more choices.

PART 4

Start-Up and Shut-Down

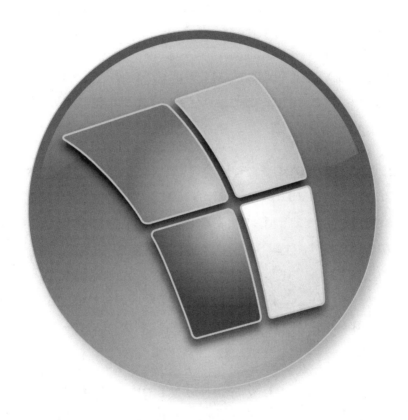

What Is Booting Up The Computer?

Booting Up is a term for starting your computer. It initiates an automatic routine that clears memory, (the computer's, not yours!), loads the operating system, and prepares the computer for use.

To start the computer:

If this is your first start-up, make a quick check of the cables and plugs to make sure they are all connected.

Check the floppy-disk drive (if you have one) to be sure it is empty. The computer is looking for instructions to start-up. It will take the instructions either from the floppy drive or internal hard drive. If a floppy that is not a start-up disk is in the "A" drive, your PC will display a "non-system disk or disk error" message; and it will not boot up.

Relax, it's not a big deal. Just push the eject button and remove the floppy and then press the Spacebar.

What Is Booting Up The Computer?, Cont.

Next, flip on the surge protector switch, or turn on the computer and monitor power switches. You may hear the machine begin to grumble and grind, and various lights may blink. You'll probably hear a beep. At about the same time you will see some technical messages scrolling by. This is normal. And no, you do not need to read those messages.

Generally, the pointer on the Windows Desktop turns into a spinning circle while it is booting up. When the pointer comes back on steady, your computer is ready for use.

What Should I See On The Screen After Start-Up?

When there are multiple users of a computer, the first screen you will see is a "user" selection screen. Each person will have their own settings for appearance, themes, choices and passwords. Select your user icon and your settings will appear.

After the start-up, what you should see on the monitor is the Windows Desktop. It is your home base, like the physical desk where your computer sits. Several tools to get you started are placed on the background area. These include a Taskbar, sidebar, icons, and a Start button.

There will be variations from computer to computer on what the Desktop looks like. You will be able to customize the look of your Desktop to suit your artistic feelings!

A Customized Desktop

How Do I Switch Users If The Computer Is Already Running?

Switching between users is easy.

- Click the Start Button.
- In the bottom right corner of the Start Menu, Click the Right Arrow.
- Now click Switch Users. A list of users will pop up.
- Select your User Name, insert your password and either press Enter on the keyboard or click the arrow to the right of the password. Windows Vista will come up with all of your user settings and preferences.

What Is The Welcome Center?

When you first start your computer, Microsoft has pre-programmed a Welcome Center to pop up as the first open window. The Vista Welcome Center is a great way to learn about Vista, your computer and all you can do with it. There are tutorials that will teach you how to go onto the Internet, store photos, listen to music and much, much more.

It is also a great place to get help if you need some questions answered. Generally, every program has a help menu that you can do some research to solve any problems you are having.

When you no longer want to have the Welcome Center pop up upon start-up, simply check the box at the bottom of the screen that says not to show it any more. You can always access the Welcome Center from the Start Menu.

What Is A Window?

A window is a framed region on your screen. It is a rectangular pane with information in it. You can have a number of windows open at any one time. You can navigate from window to window simply by clicking on the border of any of the windows you want to see.

Just like a real window, you can open and close them at any time.

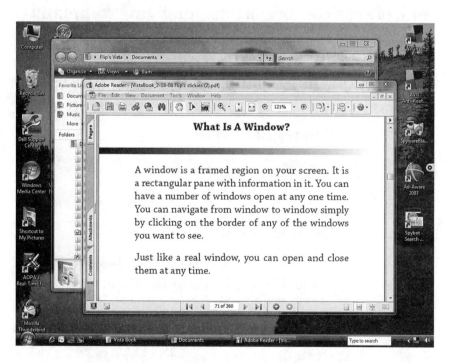

A Window Used While Writing This Book

What Are The Parts Of A Window?

Each window has a Title Bar at the top. It usually has the program name and the name of the document you are working on displayed in it.

The Menu Bar is located directly under the title bar. It displays a list of command categories. In each category of commands, there are a number of choices.

The Toolbar is usually located under the menu bar. It displays a row of buttons for giving commands.

At the bottom of the window might be additional information. For example, in a word processing program, there might be information on word count, pages, paragraphs etc.

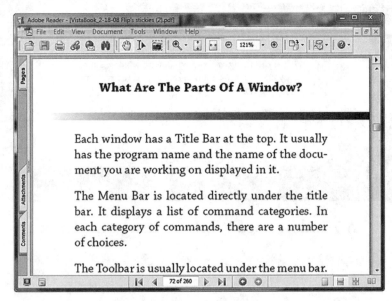

What Are The Taskbar Buttons?

The Taskbar is the bar at the bottom of the Desktop. The Taskbar Buttons launch programs just like clicking on a desktop icon.

The Start Button is on the left side of the task bar. It has the Microsoft logo on it and if you place the pointer there, the word Start will appear. For most buttons, if you hover your pointer over them, you'll get more information about what that button is.

Just to the right of the Start button are Quick Launch Buttons. These act like shortcuts to programs you use frequently.

Program Buttons appear on the middle of the Taskbar to identify any open applications or programs currently being used along with the documents you are working on. On the right side of the Taskbar you will see programs that start automatically when you start Windows. On the far right you will see the time displayed.

If a program is minimized (meaning it does not appear on the screen, but is still running), clicking on it from the Taskbar brings it back on-screen. You can easily switch to a different window by clicking its program button on the Taskbar.

A new feature of Vista is the Aero Button just to the right of the start button. Clicking the Aero button allows you to easily switch between open windows on your desktop, and then select the one you want to work with. It's a pretty cool shortcut to help you keep organized while you are working. Not all versions of Vista have the Aero button.

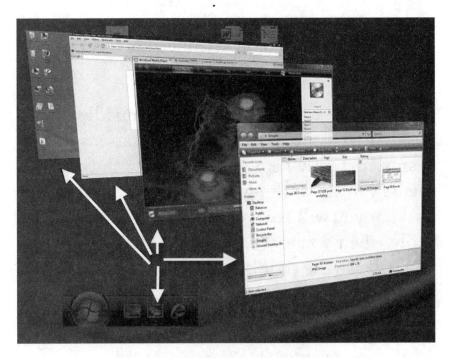

After Clicking the Aero Button

What Is The Start Button?

The Start Button is the button that takes you al-most everywhere in Windows. It is located on the Taskbar. Clicking on the Start button brings up a single menu from which many menus and pro-grams can be accessed.

To display the Start menu, click the Start button. You will see the following window:

Clicking the Start Button Opens the Start Menu

What Is The Help And Support System?

Not only can you get help from The Welcome Center, but Vista offers boatloads of help via the Help and Support Menu.

- Click on Start
- Click Help and Support

You will be taken to an area where you can find out information about how to use your computer, or solve a problem.

Some of the help features require you to be able to go out onto the Internet. Make sure you are connected to the Internet before you try to find support out there.

What Is Search Help?

Search Help is a tool to quickly find the information you need to solve a problem.

After you click Help and Support, a window appears and at the top is a rectangular typing box with "Search Help" in it. Place your curser there and type a topic you want to get help with. Press Enter on your keyboard.

A list of possible solutions/answers to your question will appear in a new window. Click on one of the topics and you will be able to read about that topic.

Keep in mind that the computer help function cannot read minds. You may have to modify your request a bit until you get the information you are looking for.

What Is Guided Help?

Once you ask for help, you may get more than just information. You may get the steps to solve your issue. Simply click on the links as they come up (words highlighted in blue) and follow the instructions.

Sometimes, you are offered an automatic solution to your problem. The computer will fix the issue for you. For the most part, these automatic fixes work great.

During this process, you may be asked questions pertaining to your issue. Once again, the computer is not a mind reader. It is just looking for information from you so it can apply the best solution.

What Is Product Activation?

When you first turn on your new computer, you will need to activate your Microsoft product. You will need to be able to go out onto the Internet to do this.

Product activation verifies that you have a valid copy of Vista and identifies you as the user. Once you are activated, you will have full use of Microsoft's Web sites to learn more about your computer and to keep it up to date with software improvements.

This is important to keep your computer healthy and running trouble free.

Should I Turn Off My Computer When I'm Not Using It?

There are a number of schools of thought about this. One says that computers are pretty reliable so why turn them off. That way they are ready to go whenever you are: no booting up process to go through.

Another says that if you're not using them, why waste the power to run them (although they do not use much power at all). Also, if unattended, someone could get access to your computer without your knowledge.

In the big scheme of things, whatever makes you comfortable, do it.

When Do I Re-Start My PC?

Every once in awhile your PC may experience a puzzling failure. It may just freeze up for no reason at all. DO NOT WORRY! YOU DID NOT DO IT! It is just the nature of computers to get confused on occasion. When this happens, your mouse will stop responding, the keyboard is not functional and the computer just sits and stares at you. That pesky machine just won't respond to your inputs. You will need to restart the computer.

First, try to shutdown the frozen program. Click the X in the upper right hand corner of the window. If that does not work, press these three keys at the same time: CTRL, ALT and DEL.

Find the frozen program in the list, select it and click End Program.

If that did not work, Click the Start button, then Click the lower right arrow, then Restart Computer.

If that did not work, an alternate method is to press and hold the CTRL and ALT keys, then press the DEL key three times.

If that did not work, here's the last ditch method. Turn off the power button on the computer. Let it rest for a minute or so and then turn it back on. On a number of computers, you must hold in the power button until the computer shuts down.

Another reason to restart a computer is if you have loaded a new program. Sometimes Windows requires a restart for all the new settings to take effect. In this case, just use the Start Menu Restart procedure. Sometimes, the new program will offer to restart the computer for you.

PART 5

Basic Controls and Skills

What Basics Skills Do I Need?

Basic skills are used repeatedly in every program. They include selecting text, cutting, copying, pasting and deleting text. You will also need to know how to open, close, save and print a document.

Selecting Text. Click at the beginning of the text you want to select. Hold down the mouse button and drag to the end of the text you want. Release the button and your text is highlighted.

Cutting and Copying Text. Once you have selected some text, you can Cut or Copy the selection and use it elsewhere. If you want to use the text elsewhere, but leave it in its original position, use the Copy command. If you want to remove the text for use elsewhere, use the Cut command. Use either the Edit drop down menu from the Tool Bar or a right mouse click to find these two editing tools. Select the one you want. What you are doing with either command is putting this text selection on "The Clipboard." The Clipboard stores this text for your use in the editing process.

Pasting. Once you have Cut or Copied your text, then move the cursor to where you want to insert the text, and go back to the Edit menu and click Paste.

Deleting Text. Deleting text is different than Cutting text. If there is a selection of text you want to eliminate, and you do not want to use it again, use the Delete key rather than Cut. Deleted text is not stored on the clipboard as is Cut or Copy text.

Saving a document. One of the most important precautions you can take while working is to save your work frequently. To save your work, click on File and then Save. The first time you do this a Save dialog box will appear. If the default name is not a good name for your document, type in a name you like better. Then click Save. Most programs have a disk icon on the toolbar which is also a save command. The Save As command allows you to make a copy of a document and rename it. This allows you to change the document yet still save an original copy.

Printing your work. From the File Menu, choose Print. After making sure all of the options are set the way you want them, click OK.

There is generally a Quick Print icon on the Program Menu Bar. It looks like a little printer. This will start the printing process without going to the printer options dialog box.

How Do I Open A File Or Program?

To open any file or program, simply find its icon on the computer, or its name from a list of programs, and click on it.

When you open a file or a program, a window will open to show you what you've asked for. If you have clicked on a file, say a letter to a friend, not only do you see this letter, but the program you created it with opens as well. Therefore if you are working in a program, you will have at least two windows open: the program window and the document window.

How Do I Move A Window?

You may want to rearrange where a window is located on your desktop. Follow these steps to move a window:

- Place the pointer on the window's title bar.
- Drag the title bar to the location you want and release the mouse button.

This will not work if your window is in full screen mode. Full screen means this one window takes up all the space on your monitor. You need to reduce the size of the window in order to be able to move it around.

A Reduced Window

What Is Minimizing, Restoring And Closing A Window?

While working in an open window, you might want to temporarily hide it to work on something else. You can send the window to the Taskbar by either clicking the Minimize Button in the upper right hand corner of the window, or clicking its Taskbar button on the Taskbar.

The Minimize button is the square with a dash in it representing a smaller window size.

To restore the window to the desktop, simply click on its Taskbar button and it will come back to the desktop.

Running programs that you are not working in takes up precious memory resources. When you are done working with a document or program, save your work and then close the file or program. You can close a file by clicking the Close Button in the upper right hand corner of the window. The close button is red with a white 'X'. You can also close the file by clicking on File in the upper tool bar and then Exit.

What Is Minimizing, Restoring And Closing A Window?, Cont.

In many Microsoft programs, rather than File being displayed in the upper left toolbar, a Microsoft logo is displayed. Many functions that we used to find under File will be found there.

The button between the minimize button and the close button in the upper right hand corner of a window is a Sizing Button. You can click it and a full screen presentation will get smaller, but not minimize. To go back to the full screen, click it again. You should notice that when you are in full screen, the button has two little windows displayed. When you are in the little window, a single full size icon is in the button.

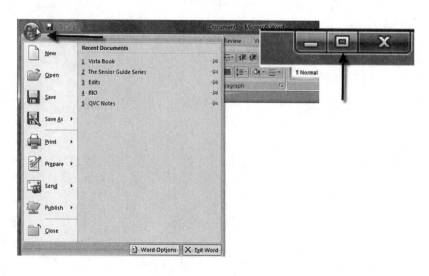

Window Buttons

How Do I Switch Between Windows?

To look at a window that is not on top of the stack, either click on the window you want, click on its Taskbar button or click on the Aero quick launch button and then select the window you want.

When you select the window by any of these methods, the window will jump to the top of the stack.

The re-sizing button discussed on the last page allows you to 'look behind' the document you are working on.

How Do I Re-Size A Window?

You may want to change the size of a window to make it easier to read, or to have more than one window side by side on the desktop. There are several ways to re-size a window.

Put the pointer on any of the window's borders, but not on the title bar. The mouse pointer turns into a two-headed arrow. Drag the border to change the size of the window. If the pointer does not change to the double-headed arrow, make sure you are not in full screen mode. Click the upper right re-size button and then try finding the two-headed arrow.

Put the pointer on any of the corners of the window. The mouse pointer again turns into a two-headed arrow. Drag diagonally and the window reduces in size both vertically and horizontally.

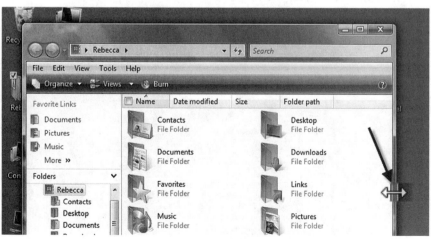

Resizing A Window

What If I Have Too Many Open Windows?

There are some commands you can use to "clean-up" the window clutter on your Desktop.

- Right-click the mouse anywhere on the Taskbar and a menu appears.
- Select Cascade. The Cascade command displays the windows so that the title bars of each window appear.
- Click on the title bar to bring its window to the front of each stack.
- Show Windows Stacked displays each window in horizontal panes and the Show Windows Side by Side displays each window in vertical panes.
- Click the Aero Quick Launch button to stack the windows for easy viewing.
- You can always close a window once you are finished working with it.

What Is A Menu?

A menu is a list of commands or options displayed on your screen, which allows you to perform a myriad of tasks.

Just as you would select your choices from a restaurant menu, you select the choices of what to do on your computer.

The most frequently used menu is the Start Menu. All of your programs and files are easily accessed from here.

Each program has its menus for doing all sorts of tasks.

When you click on any menu, a small box opens giving you optional commands to work with. Once you have selected an option from a menu, another box may appear. That's called opening a sub-menu. These are small windows that open and close as you use them. You are being given more options on how to do your task at hand.

A menu bar is an on-screen display that lists available categories of commands. It is usually located at the top of the program window. To choose a category or command, just click on it.

How Do I Use Menus And Sub-Menus?

It is as simple as this:

On the menu bar, choose the category of the command that you want. The menu opens.

Click on the command you want. Voila!

If a sub-menu opens, it is just giving you more options of how to accomplish your task at hand. Find what you want and once again click on it.

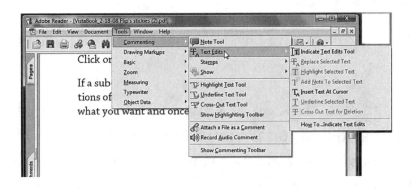

A Tool Menu With Sub-Menus

What Is A Dialog Box?

A dialog box is an on-screen message box or window that enables you to choose options and send other information to a program. It conveys information to, or requests information from the user.

The computer does its best to do what you want it to. When it is asked to do something and it needs more information, it starts a dialog with you to see what your intentions are. The dialog box gives you control over how the computer does your tasks.

Sometimes the computer thinks it has enough information to do what you want and it goes its merry way. You can always initiate the dialog so that the computer will do what you want it to.

What Is A Scroll Bar?

A scroll bar is a gray rectangle with small black arrows on both ends. It is on the right side of a window for vertical scrolling and on the bottom for horizontal scrolling.

When a document is so big it cannot be completely displayed on the monitor, a scroll bar appears. You can see the entire document by moving the scroll indicator up and down the screen, or right and left.

By clicking the up/down scroll arrow one time, you will move the document one line at a time.

Clicking on a blank spot above or below the scroll indicator, you will move the document up/down one page. You can continuously scroll by depressing the mouse button steadily instead of just clicking it.

To move the document with keyboard strokes, use the Page Up and Down Keys.

Scrolling Using The Scroll Bars

Can I Arrange Icons On The Desktop?

You can arrange your icons any way you want. Put your pointer on each icon you want to move. Click and hold down the left mouse button and drag the icons where you want them.

Then on a blank spot on the desktop, right click the mouse. Select View and then uncheck Auto Arrange and Align to grid. Your icons should stay put.

By clicking Auto Arrange, the computer will put them where it thinks they should go. With Align to Grid, they will be stacked neatly on the desktop.

I like to put my anti-virus icons on the right side to remind me to run my scans. I keep the documents that I am working on in the middle of the desktop. I keep the Computer, Recycle Bin and other frequently used icons on the left side.

What Is A Shortcut Menu?

A shortcut menu, or alternate menu is a hidden menu that can be shown with a right-click of the mouse. Almost every object on your computer has one. These are frequently used commands that are made easy to get to with one right-click.

The commands vary from program to program so you should right click in every program you use to get an idea of what commands are at "your fingertips".

Shortcut Menu of Windows Media Center

What Are The Function Keys?

On your keyboard, there are a number of keys with special functions. Laptop keyboards are slightly different than desktop keyboards, but all the functions should still be there.

Key	What It Does
F1–F12	These are programmable keys called function keys. They provide special functions depending on the software you are using.
Esc	The escape key cancels a command or an operation.
Numeric Keypad	A calculator-style, set of keys for entering numbers.
NumLock	The Number Lock key switches the right-hand keypad between typing numbers and being used as cursor keys.
Arrow Keys	The keys that move the cursor onscreen. The arrow keys move the cursor in the direction indicated by the arrow on each key-one character left or right or one line up or down.
Page Up (PgUp) and Page Down (PgDn)	These keys move the cursor to the preceding screen (PgUp) or the next screen (PgDn).
Ctrl	The control key pressed in combination with other keys, acts as a shortcut to execute commands and to select commands from the drop down menus.
Delete (Del)	This key deletes the current character.

Basic Skills Review

- "Click" means one quick press and release of the left mouse button.
- "Double click" means two quick press and releases of the mouse button.
- "Right click" means one quick press and release of the right mouse button.
- Highlighting (or selecting text) means placing the cursor at the beginning of the text, holding the left mouse button down, and dragging the cursor to the end of your desired selection and releasing the mouse button.
- Copy and cut are editing tools where you can reuse text. Delete is an editing tool that removes text permanently.
- Practicing daily improves mouse and keyboard skills.

PART 6

Understanding Windows Explorer

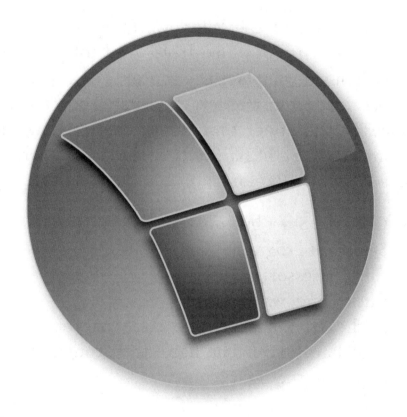

What Is Windows Explorer?

Windows Explorer is a method of seeing everything on your computer. You look at the contents through a single window in a hierarchical structure.

The left side of the Windows Explorer window contains a list of your drives and folders, and the right side displays the contents of any folder you select from the left side list. You can use View in the upper tool bar to change how the icons on the right half of the window appear. To use Windows Explorer:

- Click the Start button.
- Select All Programs.
- Click Accessories.
- Click Windows Explorer.
- In the left pane, click the letter that represents your hard drive. The hard drive contents will appear in the right pane.

What Is The Computer Icon?

The Computer Icon (labeled My Computer in earlier Windows versions) is another way to view the entire contents of your computer. It allows you to browse drives, directories (folders) and files.

Unlike Windows Explorer which shows you the contents in a hierarchical structure, clicking on the Computer Icon shows you the contents of a single folder or drive.

For Example, if you click on the Computer Icon either on the desktop or in the Start Menu, you will see the next level of folders and files that are stored there. That level includes your hard drive, your removable drives and maybe a few folders. Obviously your computer holds more than that.

After Clicking the Computer Icon

Click on the hard drive and now you see the contents of the hard drive. Keep working through your drive until you find the folder or file you want.

After Clicking the C: Drive

Which Way Should I Explore My Drives?

It does not matter whether you look through your drives with Windows Explorer or My Computer. You will get the same results. However, you will gravitate to the method you like best. I like Windows Explorer while my husband likes My Computer.

The reason you may want to look through the drives is to see the entire contents of a drive, find lost folders or documents, or move files around. There is a lot you can accomplish by looking through the filing architecture of your computer.

What Is The Address Bar?

The Address Bar displays the location "trail" for your file. It shows the file's location in hierarchal format all the way back to the hard drive. But it also allows you to jump to any of the locations displayed in the address bar.

Prior to Clicking Documents

In the above picture, if you clicked on Documents, you would be shown a list of files in the Documents Folder. Click on one of those, and you will go there.

This is just another way to navigate around your computer.

What About Folder Contents?

When you start working with Windows Explorer, you will be looking at folders. When you click on a folder, you will be looking at the folders inside that folder. You continue to look down into the filing structure until you find the file you want to work with. This might be a document, a photo or a music file. To the computer, they are all the same: just files.

Once you find the file you are looking for, you can easily see where it is located by looking at the address bar.

How Do I Change Views?

There are a number of ways to look at each and every document, file or folder. You control this with the View Menu. For example, you might want your photos in a large icon format. This will give you a preview of each of your photos while still in the folder view. For documents, you may want a title list instead. You can choose your views for each and every folder from the View menu.

To change how you view inside any Folder, click on the View Tab on the toolbar. Then adjust the settings as necessary.

The Organize Button also provides you with ways to adjust how your folders look and react.

What Are Folder Options?

You can change how you see your folders just as you can modify your desktop. You get choices everywhere with Windows Vista!

Open a folder, and click on Organize. A Folder Options dialog box opens. From here you can make adjustments to how your folders look and act.

For both sorting and folder options, you will need to play around a bit.

One recommendation is to click on Show Hidden Files and Folders. You never know when you are going to need to find something that is normally hidden. It's a good idea to be set up for it now.

How Can I Customize My Folders Look?

You can "dress up" your folders by adding a picture or icon to any folder. Simply find a folder you want to customize. Then right click on a blank spot of the folder. Then click Customize. You'll be brought to a dialog box where you can browse your computer and place a picture on the folder cover.

Once again, you'll need to play around a bit to get used to "massaging" your computer to the way you want it.

How Do I Sort?

While working in Windows, you can sort any folder in a number of different ways. By looking at the header bar, you will see various criteria that Windows can sort by. Want to see the folder list by when you last worked in the folders? Simply sort via the Date Modified header.

Want a reverse alphabetical listing, click the Name header, then the arrow to change from ascending to descending (or back).

Windows Explorer Review

- Windows Explorer actually manages the Start Menu, Taskbar, and Welcome Center.
- Windows Explorer allows you to see what is stored on each drive, in each directory and in each folder.
- As long as you name files and folders logically, you will always be able to find them, even if you misplace them.
- Windows Explorer cannot find items that went to the Recycle Bin, if you've already thrown out the trash (emptied the Recycle Bin).

PART 7

Basics for Managing Files and Folders

How Do I Find Files Or Folders?

When you are looking for a particular folder or file, and you are not sure where it is located on your computer, you can use the Search command instead of opening numerous folders. The Search command lets you quickly search a specific drive or your entire computer. To find a file or folder:

- Click the Start Button, click on Search. The Search dialog box appears.
- In the Search box on the right, type the file or folder name you want to find.
- You can narrow down the search by using the Show Only search bar. Click that category if you want to only show those results.
- Click Enter. The results of the search will appear. You can use Advanced Search if you want to tailor your search results.

A word to the wise: start filing your information in an orderly manner at the beginning of your computer experience. It will make life easier!

How Do I Open A File or Folder?

After you have located the file you want, either through a search or by going straight to it in a directory, you can double-click on it to open it.

To find and open a file or folder without using Search:

- On the Desktop, double-click Computer.
- Double-click the drive that contains the file or folder you want to open.
- Double-click the file or folder.

If you have recently opened a file that you want to look at again, check Documents or Recent. You can also open files and folders from the File Open command in the application itself. For example, if you are working in Microsoft Word, you can find other Word created documents by using the File Open method. A list of your Word documents will show up.

How Do I Create A File Or Folder?

To create a folder:

- On the Desktop, double-click Computer.
- Double-click the disk drive or folder in which you want to create a folder. The drive or folder opens.
- On the Organize menu, click Create New Folder.

An alternate way is to:

- Right-click a blank area in any window.
- Click New.
- Click Folder and it will appear.

While the "New Folder" title is highlighted, type a folder name of your choice and then press Enter. The new folder appears in the location you selected.

What Are File Properties?

File properties are the attributes of a particular file. This includes location, size, date created and much, much more.

To access any file's Properties box, right click on the file's icon, or if the file is open, click on the File menu, then Properties.

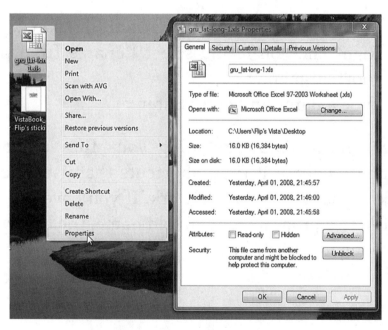

**After Clicking Properties,
the File Properties Box Opens**

How Do I Rename A File Or Folder?

It is simple to rename a file or folder. To rename:

- In a window, select the file or folder you want to rename.
- On the Organize menu, click Rename.
- Type a name and press Enter.

Or

- Select the file or folder you want to rename.
- Right click on it and select Rename from the shortcut menu.
- Type a name and press Enter.

Be careful about renaming your files without thinking about it first. Shortcuts that use an old file name will no longer work. If you have linked a file to a program with an old name, the link will no longer work either.

How Do I Copy Or Move Files Or Folders?

There are two simple ways to copy or move files and folders.

You can right-click on a file or folder, then select Copy. Then go to where you want the copy to appear, right-click, then select Paste. A copy of the original folder will appear.

For moving, right click the file or folder and then click Send To. Select from the list of likely locations.

To move a file you can also drag its icon from one location to another. Open the folder that holds your file or folder that you want to move. Also open the destination folder. Re-size both windows so they both appear on your desktop. Click on the target file or folder, hold down the mouse button and drag it to the destination folder. The icon will disappear from the original folder and appear in the new folder.

What Does It Mean To Burn To Disc?

To burn a disc simply means to make a copy. You could be copying music from your computer to a CD so you can play some tunes in your car. You could also be backing up your checkbook files. This is also known as burning. The term is used whether you are copying to a CD or DVD.

Vista makes it easy to burn files. Simply select the file you want to copy, and click on the Burn button on the toolbar. Follow the instructions.

Make sure you have the correct discs for the type of drives you have. You cannot burn a DVD in a CD drive.

How Do I Delete Files And Folders?

To Delete a file or folder, you can:

- Right-click on the icon.
- Then select Delete.

This will send the file or folder to the Recycle Bin.

Alternately, you can click on the icon and drag it to the Recycle Bin.

How Do I Use The Recycle Bin?

The Recycle Bin is just another folder that holds the files and folders you want to permanently delete. However, just like the trash at home, you have to "take it out" to really get rid of them.

Until you empty the recycle bin, the files and folders can be moved back to wherever you want them. This way you do not have to worry about sending things to the recycle bin and then wondering if you should not have thrown them out.

To get something out of the Recycle Bin, click on the Recycle Bin Icon. Either click on Restore All, or right-click on an individual file/folder and select Restore.

To empty the Recycle Bin, right-click on its icon and select Empty Recycle Bin. Or, if you are in the recycle bin, click the Empty Recycle Bin button on the toolbar. Now your files really are deleted.

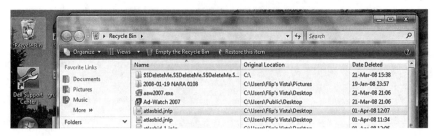

Part of the Recycle Bin

What Are File Conflicts?

File conflicts exist when you try to name two different files with the same name. If you are creating the second file, Vista will warn you when you try to save a file name that already exists. Vista will offer three possible solutions: Copy and Replace, Don't Copy, and Copy But Keep Both Files. Make sure you read the selections and pick the one that is most appropriate for what you want.

You should normally name each file with separate, specific names. For example, a lettertoson.doc should not be used for every letter to your son. The next letter could be lettertoson2.doc, lettertoson3.doc etc.

If you make a copy of the file named lettertoson.doc, the copy will be titled lettertoson.doc (copy1). That way you can have this one letter appear as different files.

What Are Recent Items?

Recent Items are files you have been working with lately. They might be individual letters, photos, documents, etc. Via the Start Menu, you can quickly see a list of those Recent Items and open them.

To see that list, click on Start, then from the list on the right side of the Start Menu, click Recent Items. A list of your recently looked at items will pop up. Then click on the item you want and it will open.

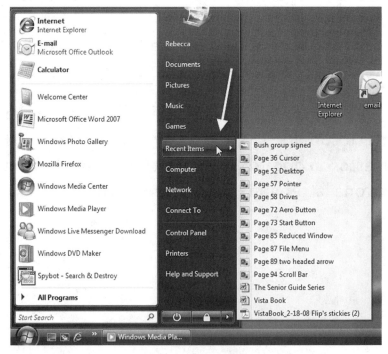

Recent Items

What Are Compressed Folders?

Compressed folders hold files that have been re-duced in size so they take up less room on your disks. They are known as "zipped" folders and have a little zipper on the icon. These folders have not lost any important information from your files, but through some "propeller head" technol-ogy, they've squeezed the files down in size as you would a sponge.

Most users do not need to compress files and fold-ers. However, if you find you need to, read on.

To compress files, simply create a new compressed folder by right clicking on an empty area of a window, then New, Compressed (zipped) Folder. A new folder will appear. Name this new folder. Then drag your files that you want to compress to this new folder. Now they're compressed.

To get them back from being compressed, just drag them to a non-compressed folder and they will come back. However, a compressed copy will remain in the compressed folder.

If someone sends you a compressed file, simply drag it out of the compressed folder and it will "reconstitute" itself.

Again, most folks will not need to compress files. Most new computers have plenty of disk space for most everything you'll ever do with a computer.

How Do I Play A CD?

Playing music with the CD Player is very simple. A feature called auto-play detects when you insert a CD into the CD drive and automatically starts the music for you.

If auto-play does not work, here is how to do it manually. Follow these steps to play a CD:

- Click the Start button.
- Select All Programs.
- Select Windows Media Player.
- Select the CD title in the list on the left.
- Select the song title in the right pane.

You do not have to use Windows Media Player. If you have a different player on your computer, follow their instructions for their product. Other players include iTunes, Real Player and Adobe Media Player, just to name a few.

How Do I Play Media Clips And Movies?

Playing any media format is easy with Windows Media Player. Open the player as you did on the previous page by going to Start, All Programs and then Windows Media Player (or click the Windows Media Player icon).

On the File Menu, click Open. Then Browse and locate the file you want to view or hear. Click on that and it should start playing.

If you receive a media file via e-mail, it probably played just fine when you clicked on it. However, if you try to find it while it is still in your e-mail inbox via a media player, you might not find it. If this happens, save the media file to a folder outside of your e-mail program.

What Is The Windows Media Center?

This is a more advanced version of Windows Media Player, but is only offered with Vista Home Premium and Ultimate editions.

Not only can you play CDs and DVDs, but Windows Media Center will catalog all digital media content on your computer to give you a one-stop viewing location for videos, movies, photos and much more.

In addition, with the correct hardware added, you can listen to FM radio broadcasts and even watch TV on your computer monitor.

When you first start Windows Media Center, you will need to run a setup program. Express Setup works best for most users.

What Is A Screen Saver?

A screen saver is a program that displays an image or animation on your screen when your PC is idle.

It was invented to insure that all parts of the monitor screen received equal amounts of illumination so a ghost image would not be "burned" onto the screen. Today's monitors don't have burn-in problems and screen savers are not really necessary, but almost everyone uses them anyway.

Screen savers are fun and often entertaining. You can use any number of pre-installed screen savers or you can use screen savers downloaded from the Internet. You can even use any of your saved digital photos.

How Do I Get A Screen Saver?

Vista comes with many screen savers as part of the package. There are many more screen savers available commercially. To find the screen savers included with Vista:

- Right-click on a blank spot on the Desktop and choose Personalize to open the display properties dialog box.
- On the Screen Saver link, select an option from the drop-down list.
- Click OK to make this your screen saver.

To use images you have stored on your computer as your screen saver, simply pick Photos as your screen saver option.

What Is A Font?

According to <u>Answers.com</u>, a font is "A complete set of type of one size and face." It is a selectable style of printing. Some examples:

I like this font.

I like this font.

I like this font.

Or even,

I LIKE THIS FONT.

As you can see, every style is different. You should pick a style you like, but one that is easily readable by others. Some fonts may cause eye strain as they can be difficult for some folks to read.

What Is The Character Map?

There are many symbols, letters and numbers within a font type that the keys of a keyboard cannot display. You might want to use a Greek letter, or a Russian numeral.

To find these, simply:

- Click on Start.
- In the Search Box start typing Character Map and it will appear at the top of the Start Menu.
- Click on Character Map.
- Select the Font you are working with, then scroll down to find the character you are looking for. Select it.
- Then click Copy.
- Go back to your document and Paste the character(s) where you want it.

How Do I Add A Printer?

Adding a printer to your computer is easy. Simply connect the printer cable to your computer, and turn on the printer. The computer should recognize that a new piece of equipment as been added. If it does not, restart your computer.

After the computer has configured itself for this new printer, it will tell you it is ready to go.

Sometimes the computer can get confused and might ask you for an installation disk. All new printers come with one so you should have it ready just in case you need it. If you are asked for the installation disk, insert it into the correct drive and the computer should get the information it needs from the disk.

How Do I Print A Document?

From the File Menu, choose Print. After making sure all of the options are set the way you want them via the Print Properties dialog box, click OK.

There is generally a Quick Print icon on the Program Menu Bar. It looks like a little printer. This will start the printing process without going to the printer options dialog box.

What Is Print Preview?

Print Preview is an easy way to view your document before it is printed. Click on Print Preview and your document is shown as it will appear in print. If you do not like something about the print job, you can go back and adjust the document before printing.

Want to check on how that special character you picked will look? Use the zoom bar and take a look. Do the margins look okay on all the pages? This is how you can check before it goes to print.

What Is A Printer Configuration?

You can set up default settings for your printer so that it plans on printing the same way every time. You can still make changes for each document that you create, but it will be from these default settings.

To change these settings:

- Click on Start.
- Then Control Panel.
- Then Printers.
- Right-click on your printer.
- Select Printer Preferences. Make your adjustments here.

You can also exercise some control via the Properties option after you right click on your printer. Mostly, you would use this to share a printer on a network.

Files And Folders Review

- Keep a logical filing system starting on Day One.
- Use folders to store similar files.
- It does not matter if it is a piece of writing, a photo, or a piece of music, if it's stored on your computer, it's still a file.
- When printing, you will always have the option to adjust printing properties if you print from a file or print menus via a quick print icon.

PART 8

Programs

What Is A Program?

Program is synonymous with software. It is a set of instructions, written in programming language that a computer can execute to perform your tasks in a certain way.

Windows Vista comes with four types of programs:

Accessory programs — Located in the Accessories folder in the Program menu. They include: Accessibility, Communications, Entertainment, Games, System Tools, Calculator, Imaging, Keyboard Manager, Notepad and Wordpad.

Control Panel programs — The control panel allows you to adjust how all of the pieces/parts of your computer work. You will find these programs by clicking the Start button and then selecting Control Panel.

Pre-loaded Software — May include word processing, financial management or digital imagery.

What Is A Program?, Cont.

MS_DOS prompt — MS_DOS refers to the typed code used to make the computer do its work. Windows uses a graphical representation of the MS-DOS code, which is a great improvement in user-friendliness. Do not worry about this function. It is rarely used these days.

Although many books still give you instructions on MS_DOS, we will not refer to it in this book. If you get advanced enough to use MS_DOS so that you can look "under the hood," an in-depth MS_DOS book will be better for you.

Can I Add New Programs?

Eventually, you will probably think to yourself, "I'll bet there is a specialized program to help me do this task?" You bet there is!

However, before you buy a new program, make sure that you can run that program on your system. Check the system requirements (printed on the side of the software box). These include type of microprocessor, amount of memory, hard disk space, video card, other required equipment and whether or not it is Vista compatible.

Today, most software ships on CD or DVD discs. You must have the correct drive.

Software can also be purchased and downloaded from the Internet. No need to go to the store! Simply follow the instructions from the vendor's Web site. Warning! Make sure you know who you are downloading from before you purchase a program via the Internet!

How Do I Add A New Program?

To add a program:

- Insert the installation disc in the drive. If you are installing from a disk that has an Auto Run feature, when you insert the disk, the installation program starts automatically.
- If the installation prompt does not come up automatically:
  - Click the Start button, select Run, and type in the drive letter the disk is in. Click OK.
  - Double-click the installation icon which looks like a CD and a box.
  - Follow the on-screen instructions.

If the installation instructions on the box differ from what you just read, follow the manufacturers recommendations.

How Do I Remove A Program?

The best way to uninstall a program is by using the Programs and Features icon, located in the Control Panel.

It is not a good idea to simply delete the program folder from Computer Icon or Windows Explorer. The original program installation may have put files in other folders and changed some of the system settings.

To remove a program:

- Click the Start button.
- Select the Control Panel.
- Double-click the Programs and Features icon.
- Select the program you want to uninstall.
- Select either Uninstall, Change or Repair.

There are two other options in this dialog box: Change or Repair. You will rarely use them.

What Is The Classic Start Menu?

The Classic Start Menu looks like previous versions of Windows. Some folks feel more comfortable with what they are used to, so Microsoft includes that option in Vista.

The Classic Menu expands to the right as you click on choices in the Start Menu. The regular Vista Start Menu shows you the next level of choices in the Start Window itself.

To Change from one to the other, simply right click the Start button. Select Properties and then check Classic if that is what you want. Whether or not you are new to computers or upgrading from a previous version, we recommend using the new Vista version rather than the Classic version. There are more features for you with the new version that makes doing tasks easier.

What Are Start Searches?

Almost everything you might want to find through the Start Menu is available via the Start Search box. Simply start typing what you are looking for and a list will be displayed of all the possible choices based on what you have typed so far.

I mentioned the Character Map earlier in the book. That is just one example of what you can find. You can locate programs and data files just by typing in Start Search.

When you find what you are looking for, click its name in the list. That program, or data file, will open.

The Classic Start View has no Start Search option. However, there is a simple way to find programs while in Classic mode. Click on Start, All Programs and a list of all the programs opens.

How Do I Create A Shortcut?

As mentioned earlier, a shortcut is a quick way to gain access to a program or file. And it is easy to create shortcuts.

Simply find the icon of what you want to gain quick access to. Let's say, Your Memoirs. Right click on the Your Memoirs icon and select Create Shortcut. A shortcut icon appears in the folder you have open. Now drag the shortcut to the desktop and you have a quick way to launch Your Memoirs without having to go through a lot of menus.

What Is Pinning To The Start Menu?

You will notice that on the Start Menu, on the left side, there is a top and bottom section. The top section is fixed. Those programs are pinned to the Start Menu and do not leave.

However, the bottom section is for recently used programs. These will change based on your usage.

However, if you would like to keep some of those programs in the upper "always there" section, you can pin them there. To pin a program to the Start Menu, right click on the program and select, Pin To Start Menu. The program icon will shift to the upper section.

To unpin a selection, right click on a program in the pinned area, and select Unpin From Start Menu. The icon will leave the upper section.

What Is Taskbar Grouping?

As you open programs and/or documents, the Taskbar can quickly become filled up with task buttons. To keep some semblance of order there, tasks that are using the same program will be grouped together with a number in the box to let you know how many are grouped there.

For example, if you run certain virus scanning software, three or four windows might be open at any one time. Meanwhile you might want to work on a document. As the Taskbar fills up with buttons, all of the virus software windows will be grouped under one name. The document and its program will be listed in another button. Open another document with the same program and it, too, will be grouped on the Taskbar.

You can see what is listed in each button by clicking on it. You can switch to any of those windows by clicking on the name of what you want.

What Is The Start-Up Folder?

The Start-Up folder will automatically start programs that you want running as soon as you turn on your computer. There are lots of programs that start when you turn on the computer, but this folder allows you to choose something you want.

For example, if you want the calculator turned on every time you start your computer, just follow these steps.

- Find the program you want — for our example, the calculator.
- Right click on it and create a shortcut on the desktop.
- Right click the Start Button
- Select Explore, then Start-Up.
- Drag the shortcut you created to the Start-Up folder.

What Is The Task Manager?

You can keep an eye on what is going on with your computer via the Task Manager. You can see what programs and processes are running, how much of your system resources are being used, monitor performance and close programs that are not responding.

Here are two ways to get to the Task Manager:

- Simultaneously press the Ctrl, Shift and Esc keys. The Task Manager will pop up.
- Simultaneously press the Ctrl, Alt Delete keys. You will be taken to a screen that offers a number of choices. One is the Task Manager. Click that. This method is good to know if you want to log off your computer, change users or perform other tasks.

If you are a novice computer user it is best not to fool around with the processes page.

Programs Review

- Only add programs you intend to use.
- If you use certain programs regularly, you can create a shortcut to them on the desktop.
- If a program freezes and stops working, the Task Manager is a tool you can use to un-freeze the computer.
- The Taskbar keeps tabs on what programs are open on your computer.
- If you like certain programs to look differently for you when there are multiple users, you can create a separate identity so the programs work as you like them.

PART 9

Maintenance

What Is The Function of System Properties?

Want to find out more about your computer details? You can check your system properties at any time. Simply right click the Computer Icon on your desktop, then click Properties. You will get a box chock full of information about your computer.

There are other ways of finding this same information. You can go to the Control Panel and click on System and Maintenance. In the Welcome Center, simply click View Computer Details.

You might need to find this page if you are working with tech support people to solve a problem.

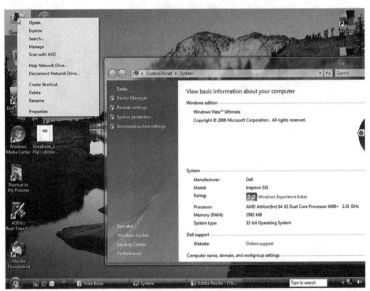

Your System Properties

Where Can I Find My PC's Performance Information?

Open the System Properties box as described on the previous page. Click Performance in the lower left corner of the box.

A new screen will open showing you various scores for system components. This is a relative scoring system and you do not need to pay much attention to it unless you are unhappy with your computer's overall performance.

From this page, you can find out information on how to improve performance in various areas. Sometimes it just requires a little housekeeping. Other solutions require spending money. Unless you absolutely have to, don't spend extra money for computer improvements that may not give you much more performance.

What Is Disk Clean Up?

Disk Clean Up is a utility function that removes unnecessary files from your computer. This should be considered a good housekeeping tool and should be done frequently. This will help keep your performance high.

To run Disk Clean Up, go to the Performance section:

- Right-click on Computer.
- Click Properties, then click Performance.
- In the left hand menu, click Open Disk Clean Up.
- Select the drive you want to clean and click on OK.

It may take a few minutes to discover all that can be deleted. When shown the results, make sure all the boxes are checked. Then click OK. All the files will be permanently deleted.

What Is Defragging?

Computers store information in clusters. However, the clusters of one file may not all be stored in the same area of the hard drive. This is normal and over time, the hard drive's ability to retrieve these clusters slows down as more and more clusters are farther and farther apart. When this happens, the disk is fragmented.

To improve performance, you can straighten up the disk and put the files back in order. This is known as Defragging.

To Defrag your disk click Start, then type in the search box Disk Defrag or just Defrag. The Disk Defragmenter dialog box will open up. To Defrag right now, click the Defragment Now button.

You will notice an area of this box that allows you to schedule Defrags for the future. See the next topic for more information.

How Do I Schedule Maintenance Tasks?

While in the Defrag box, you can set up a schedule for future defrags. Choose a time when no one is using the computer and the computer will be on. I usually use one or two o'clock in the morning. Yes, that means I leave my computer on overnight.

To set up future defrags, click the Modify Schedule button in the Disk Defragmenter box. Adjust the time and dates. Click OK.

To schedule other tasks, including maintenance tasks, go to the Task Scheduler Wizard. Click Start, then type in the Search Box Task Schedule Wizard. Click Task Schedule Wizard in the Start list. Follow the instructions within the boxes.

There are many things you can schedule with Task Scheduler. You can even remind yourself to take your daily vitamins!

What Is The Best Way To Back-Up?

The best back-up is the one that you do! I'm not trying to be flippant; backing up is important. If you back up irregularly, you are at risk of losing the information stored on your computer. If the information is not important to you, or is easily replaced from paper files, then you do not have to worry about backing up. However, most of us need the information on our computers. Daily!

I like backing up to an external hard drive. However, not everyone has one. Backing up your files to disk is fairly easy.

- Click on Start.
- Type in the Search Box Backup.
- Click Backup from the top of the list.
- Click Create copies of your files and folders.

If you are using CD or DVD discs, make sure you have the appropriate kind for your drive, and plenty of them.

Follow the on-screen directions pertaining to drive selection and start times.

What Is The Windows Security System?

The Windows Security System in Vista is a comprehensive safety tool to keep your computer free from viruses, malicious software, intentional intrusions and all the bad stuff out on the Internet. It's not foolproof, but it is the first line of defense in your computer.

To go to the Security Center, click on Start, Control Panel, then Security Center. You can also type Security Center in the Start Search Box.

Items marked in green are deemed okay. In red, yellow or orange, some attention is needed.

The areas addressed here are Windows Firewall, Windows Defender, Windows Update and Internet Options.

Windows Defender is the heart of the security system. Make sure you use Windows Defender all the time.

What Is The Windows Firewall?

A firewall keeps intruders out of your computer. You should always have one turned on. Vista has its own firewall and you should use it if you do not have another one. If you have another firewall that you want to use, great! Install it and turn it on. However, you should turn the Vista firewall off. Two firewalls running at the same time will not work well together.

From the Windows Security Center, click Windows Firewall to change settings, turn it on or off or to allow exceptions to get through the firewall.

The exceptions tab is rarely used for most home users so you should not have to deal with this.

What Is Malware Protection?

Malware harms your computer. Malware is defined as malicious software. It is software that you do not want on your computer. It generally comes via e-mail that you download onto your computer.

Malware is further delineated as spyware, adware, viruses, Trojans and any number of other nomenclature designations that will be created in the future.

Windows Defender is Vista's weapon against spyware and adware. It is automatically turned on when you turn on your computer. Windows Defender scans your computer for malware infections. By default, Windows Defender scans your computer at 2 AM. Another good reason to keep your computer on overnight. However, from the Tools menu in Windows Defender, you can adjust the scan time to suit your schedule.

What Is The Windows Update Feature?

Windows Update is a service provided by Microsoft to keep your computer in tip top condition, software wise. It will install updates to Windows and other Microsoft programs, patches for problems that arise in Microsoft programs and help keep your computer secure and performing well.

You can elect to let Microsoft update your computer automatically, or just inform you that updates are available. At The Senior's Guide, we recommend that you use the automatic feature. This means once again you should leave your computer on when you schedule Windows to update.

To set up Windows Update simply click Start, then type Update in the Search Box. Click on Windows Update in the Start Menu. The main window tells you the status of Windows Update. If this is your first time going to Windows Update, you should update your computer right away.

In the left hand section of the window are some links. Change settings is where you can customize how Windows Update works. You can elect not to update (NOT RECOMMENDED!), inform you of updates and allow you to select the ones you want, or update Automatically and at what time, and how often.

Maintenance Checklist

- Start your good housekeeping practices today.
- Keep your firewall on.
- Keep your antivirus, antispyware, antimalware programs up to date and running.
- Schedule disk clean up and defrag weekly.
- Keep Windows Vista up-to-date.
- Back up important files frequently.

PART 10

The Internet and Vista

What Is The Internet?

The Internet is a worldwide network of computers. In a network, computers "talk" to each other electronically and allow you to gather or share information from around the world.

Two types of computers make up the Internet: servers and clients. Servers store data (information, pictures, etc.) and "serve" it upon request, to computers known as clients, which is what your computer is considered.

The Internet connects millions of servers and clients around the world.

The Internet is often referred to as the Net, the Information Superhighway, cyberspace, or the World Wide Web (www).

What Is The World Wide Web?

The World Wide Web is a system for accessing information on the Internet. It is the graphical, multimedia portion of the Internet.

The Web links one Internet site to another with hypertext links. With hypertext links, you click on words that are highlighted in a passage and jump to a new location where more information on that subject is provided.

Do not expect every resource on the Internet to be accessible through the Web. To be accessible, a document must be coded with links that can be read by Web servers.

E-mail and newsgroups are not part of the Web.

Is There Bad Stuff On The Internet?

The Internet is just like anywhere else. There is information that everyone is happy to see and information that you never want to see. There are many more safe sites than unsafe sites.

The Internet allows people to meet without face-to-face contact. Wherever people congregate, there always seems to be a few bad apples in the barrel.

It is possible to block access to certain sites which are inappropriate for children. Most ISPs block the bad stuff at the server level. You can block any site from your browser. You do not have to look at anything you do not want to. You are in control and Vista helps you maintain that control.

How Can I Be Secure Using The Internet?

Always make sure your financial transactions are done over a secure server.

A secure server encrypts your information. That means that the information has been scrambled by software to make it unreadable by anyone but the receiving computer.

Web browsers Internet Explorer, Safari and Mozilla Firefox, include security features that let you know when your connection is secure and when it is not. A secure site is denoted with a locked padlock in the bottom bar of the browser window.

Be careful out there. Keep in mind that digital information is easily manipulated. Do not give out any information unless you know the receiver. Be a smart shopper.

Never give out your passwords to anyone over the Internet.

What Do I Need To Get Online?

You need four things to connect to the Internet:

- A computer.
- A modem, or other communication device to connect your computer to an ISP using your telephone line, television cable, ISDN line, or DSL or satellite dish.
- An ISP (Internet Service Provider) account.
- A Web browser, such as Internet Explorer, Safari, or Mozilla Firefox.

How Do I Get Connected?

The best options are cable, DSL or satellite access. They are known as broadband connections. They offer high speeds for a fixed monthly charge. Call your local cable TV operator/DSL provider/Satellite dish provider to find out if it is available in your area.

Another way to connect is by using a modem and dialing up through the standard telephone network. This is the cheapest, but slowest, way to connect.

If using dial-up, a second phone line dedicated for computer use can be very beneficial. If you only have one phone line, you cannot use the phone if the computer is online. And with the expense of a second line, it might be cheaper, easier and faster to get a broadband connection.

What Is A Network?

A network is a common group of computers connected together via a hardwired connection or a wireless connection.

The purpose of the network is to be able to easily share files, printers and even access to the Internet.

Most businesses, educational institutions and government organizations have computer networks. If you want to share an Internet connection or printer on the homefront, you can have a simple network as well.

The network connection can be as simple as a network cable connecting two computers together. More sophisticated networks may have routers or wireless connections to link your computers together. Your situation and needs will dictate how much network hardware to use.

What Is A Wireless Network?

A wireless network uses radio waves to connect the computers together. This is especially handy if you want your computer in one room, but your Internet access is in another. It's also handy if you have a portable computer and like to use it in various locations throughout the house.

If you have a laptop, it probably has a wireless adaptor built into it. You just need to access it and turn it on. For a desktop, you most likely will need to add on a wireless adaptor.

If your computer can "see" the wireless network, that means other people can as well. Make sure you use the encryption security protocols that come with your system to protect yourself from intruders.

What Is An ISP?

ISP stands for Internet Service Provider. It is an entity that has the communications and computer facilities that let you connect to its Internet link. Usually there is a fee for this service.

Sometimes the ISP is referred to as the host or server. A server makes files available to other computers. The client (your computer) uses software so you can perform online functions.

There are many ISPs from which to choose. There are local, national, and international providers. The local providers are usually independent and may limit their services to Internet access and e-mail. National and international providers may offer not only Internet access and e-mail, but also many members-only services and content. When looking for a provider, consider if they provide easy access to resources, services and information that is of the greatest interest to you. All providers are not equal.

Where Do I Get The Software To Access The Internet?

Usually your ISP provides the necessary software. If your provider does not provide free software maybe they are not the best provider choice.

Once you have established an account and connection, you are free to use whatever browser you want to, and whatever e-mail client that your ISP supports.

What Is A Web Browser And How To Choose One?

A Web browser is the key piece of Internet software needed to access and navigate the Web. The interface enables you to ask for and view Web pages.

Most Internet Service Providers supply a browser as part of the software. If you have Windows Vista on your computer, then you already have Internet Explorer.

Other popular browsers are Apple Safari and Mozilla Firefox. You can have more than one browser on your computer. Or you can try them all and choose the one that best suits you.

What Is A Domain Name?

A domain name identifies and locates a host computer or service on the Internet. It is the identifying title given to a system of computers. It is registered in much the same way as a company name.

The most popular domain types are usually one of the following:

.com = Company or commercial organization

.edu = Educational organization

.gov = Government body

.mil = Military site

.net = Internet gateway or administrative host

.org = Non-profit organization

Because the internet is growing rapidly, new domain suffixes have been created. Others include .info, .biz, .tv, .us., .cc, .name, .bz, .co. More will be added as needed.

Countries may have their own suffix. For example, .jp is Japan and .ca is Canada.

You are ready to log-on if you have a computer with a modem, an Internet browser, and an ISP.

There are many ways to set up a PC Internet connection due to different operating systems, PC configurations, and Web browsers.

To start Internet Explorer (IE) simply click either the IE icon on the desktop, the IE icon on the Quick Launch Toolbar or click Start and then the IE icon at the top of the Start Window.

This assumes you have an "always on" broadband connection. If you have a dialup connection, you will have to first connect to the Internet, before your browser will work. For ease of use, you can set up IE to dial up automatically whenever you launch it.

What Is A Web Page/Web Site?

A Web page is a document on the Web. Web pages can include text, pictures, animations, video and sound. They also contain links that connect you to other Web pages.

Different locations on the Web are known as Web sites. A Web site is comprised of one or more Web pages.

The Home Page of MeAndMyCaregivers.com

What Is A Home Page?

The first page of a Web site is often called a home page. It is the primary Web page for an individual, software application, or organization.

Home page also has another meaning. It refers to the page that appears when you start your browser and acts as your home base for exploring the Web.

To change your browser home page to the current page you are on, click on the icon of the little house in the lower right section of the toolbar. Then select the current page. You can have more than one home page listed here. When you do that, an additional tab will open up, essentially giving you two open browser windows. Each one will have its own home page.

You can also change the home page by clicking Tools on the toolbar, then Internet Options, and on the General tab you can type the Web address.

Another way is to first surf to the page you want, then use the above steps but instead of typing the address, select Use Current.

What Is A Home Page?, Cont.

You can have any Web page as your home page. I have my local TV station's home page as my home page, as that gives me top news stories, weather and an easy-to-use local search engine. Your ISP may have a similar set up that you can customize to your liking.

Changing Your Home Page Dialog Box

What Is Hypertext And Linking?

Web pages are written in HTML (HyperText Markup Language). They contain connections to other Web pages. These connections are embedded within the text.

A hyperlink is a signpost to take you to other Web pages with related information. It appears as an icon, graphic, image or word in a file, that when clicked with the mouse, automatically takes you to another Web page.

A link is usually underlined or displayed in a different color. The mouse pointer turns into a "hand" to show that the icon, graphic, image or word is a link.

To pursue a link, click on the highlighted text or image. You will jump to the new site. You can always return to previous sites by using the "Back Button" on the browser's toolbar.

What Is A URL?

Each Web page has a unique address called a URL: Uniform Resource Locator. It is a standardized addressing system for material accessible over the Internet. These unique individual addresses allow you to go to specific Web sites and pages.

If you know a site's URL, you can go directly to it by entering the URL in the address field of your browser and pressing Enter.

Each URL has three parts: the protocol, the host name, and the file path.

Reading from left to right identifies the domain and sub-domains within the site. The slashes are dividers that are necessary for the address. Do not insert any spaces.

Example: http://www.theseniorsguide.com

What Is The Meaning Of http And www?

http stands for hypertext transfer protocol and refers to a set of rules used by your browser to access and display Web pages.

If you see the prefix https, it signifies a secure or encrypted version of http. Most online merchants, banks, and brokerages use https as their communication method. This ensures your financial information is encrypted so others cannot read it.

www stands for the World Wide Web. This is the main avenue for information stored out on the Internet.

How Do I Navigate (Surf) The Web?

You can browse or surf the Web in several ways:

- You can open any Web page by typing its address in the Address Bar of your Web browser.
- When you are viewing a Web page, you can surf to related sites by clicking the links on the page.
- You can also use toolbar buttons to move between Web pages, search the Internet, go back a page or forward a page or to refresh a Web page's content.
- You can use a search engine to find related Web pages based on your inputs.

What Are The Internet Explorer Toolbar And Browser Buttons?

Button	What It Does
Back	Moves to a previously viewed Web page.
Forward	Moves to the next Web page.
Stop	Stops the downloading of a Web page.
Refresh	Updates the currently displayed Web page.
Home	Jumps to your home page.
Search	Opens a Web page that lists the available search engines.
Favorites	Displays a list of Web pages you have designated as your favorites.
History	Displays a list of recently visited sites.
Channels	Displays a list of channels you can select.
Fullscreen	Uses a smaller Standard toolbar and hides the Address bar so more of the screen is visible.
Mail	Opens Outlook Express or Internet News.
Print	Prints a Web page.
Edit	Opens FrontPage Express so you can edit a Web page.

How Do I Search The Web?

To search the Web you can use a search engine. A search engine is a program that allows you to locate specific information from a database.

At the search engine's home page, you will find a form to enter the search terms that you are looking for. Type the word or phrase that describes what you are looking for. The search engine then displays the matches.

Different search engines source, store, and retrieve their data differently. My favorite is Google. Others include HotBot, AltaVista, Yahoo, Infoseek, Excite, and Dogpile.

The search engine does a lot of work for you, but it cannot read minds. For example, if you put Levi's in the search parameter, hoping to find a new pair of blue jeans, don't be surprised if you get an essay on the history of indigo ink. The search engine looks for the keyword that you typed. If it is in the document, it will display it regardless of whether or not you care to learn about indigo ink.

How Do I Search The Web?, Cont.

So, to find a Web page where you can purchase a pair of Levi's, you might want to search "purchase Levi's" and see what you get. Try different searches and alter your search parameters and you will get the hang of it quickly.

Google Home Page

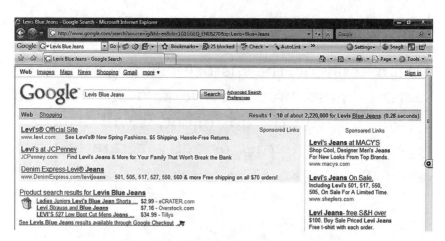

Google Search Results Page

Can I Change Search Providers?

You can use any search engine you want. Although your browser may have a search engine already attached to it, you can go to any other search engine's home page and start a search.

Vista and Internet Explorer make this easy. To the right of the search box is a little down arrow. Click that and then click Find More Providers. Pick the one you want.

Your browser may have a search toolbar attached to it. You can add another one, or turn yours off. This is your computer and for the most part, you can customize it however you want to.

To turn off a search toolbar, simply right click on the toolbar and uncheck the search engine you do not want.

To get a search engine toolbar, go to the search engine's home page and look for a download link for their toolbar.

What If I Cannot Open A Web Page?

It is just a matter of time before you click on a link or Web address that does not work. There are a couple of reasons this might happen.

If only one URL does not work, you know that it is either a wrong address, the host at its end has a problem or the address has changed or been turned off. Web addresses can change. Addresses must be exact or you will not get the site that you are looking for.

If none of the URLs work, check to make sure you have an Internet connection. If you cannot connect to any Web site, close and reopen your browser. If you still cannot connect, try restarting your computer.

Often your browser will display a pop-up window with a message and error code pointing the way to solving the problem.

What Are The Most Common Web Address Error Codes?

- **Incorrect host name.** When the address points to a nonexistent host, your browser will return an error saying, "Host not found".
- **Illegal domain name.** The illegal host name is more than likely from keying in an address with the wrong punctuation, a single slash instead of two slashes, or forgetting to put a dot after www.
- **File not found.** If the file has moved, changed names, or you have overlooked capitalization, you will get a message from the server telling you the file does not exist on the host.
- **Host refuses entry.** The host is either overloaded with traffic or temporarily off-limits and may not let you gain entry.

What Is Uploading And Downloading?

These terms refer to the flow of information into, and out of, your computer. If you send a file to another computer, you upload the file.

If you receive a file from another computer, you download it. For the most part, home users are frequent downloaders.

You can download very small files such as a thumbnail photo, or very large files such as Windows Updates. The process is all the same. Large files just take longer.

How Do I Download A File From The Web?

When you download a file, you are retrieving information from an online service onto your own computer.

When you download a file, the online service sends you a copy of the file. To retrieve it, click on the link and follow the prompts. You will be asked where on your hard drive you want to store the file and what you want to name the file.

Always look at how big the file is that you are going to download. Take into consideration how much time it will take to download. If you have a dialup connection, you probably do not want to have your telephone tied up for hours if you are expecting a call.

Organize your downloads just like the files you already have on your computer. You can download everything onto the desktop and then file them away. There is even a folder marked Downloads for you to use.

Is There An Easy Way To Return To Previously Viewed Web Sites/Pages?

Yes! You can mark the location of your favorite Web sites and pages. Internet Explorer calls it adding to your Favorites.

When you find a site that you like and want to come back to, click the Star with a Plus Sign button, (Add Favorites Button) and then click, Add To Favorites. You can now go back there with a click of the mouse. Your Favorites list will be found under the star without a plus sign.

You should organize your Favorites list right from the beginning. If not, it might be hard to find an individual favorite page from a long list. Click on the Add Favorites Button, then Organize. Create folders with meaningful titles and put like favorites into those folders.

Some browsers use the term Bookmarks instead of Favorites.

Adding a Favorite

What Are RSS Feeds?

Really Simple Syndication (RSS) is a method for automatically getting content such as blogs, news, and videos downloaded into your computer. You can view RSS content in your Web browser and can add RSS feeds easily. They are stored under the Feeds tab in your Favorites menu. Using RSS, publishers keep you current and up to date by providing content directly to you if you have subscribed to their service. For the most part, there are no fees for this service.

For example, I subscribe to two news channels' RSS feeds so I can stay on top of events all over the world. Not all Web sites have RSS feeds, but the list is growing all the time.

RSS feeds are built into many e-mail programs as well. Wherever you see a link to a feed (or the RSS icon), and you want to subscribe, just click it.

What Is Browser History?

Browser history is a list of where you have been on the Internet. You can find it in the Favorites section, under the history tab.

You can look at the history by date, by order visited and by most visited. This makes it easy to return to a page that you did not bookmark or add to your favorites list.

You can also delete your browsing history. To delete the history: Click on Tools, Internet Options and on the General Tab, Delete History. Another dialog box pops up offering to delete sections of the browsing history, or a button that says Delete All. This is a good feature to know about if you are using a public computer somewhere. You can erase your tracks, especially if you have been shopping and have used a credit card.

Remember, it is not recommended to use your credit card on a public computer.

What Is Tabbed Browsing?

With Internet Explorer 7, Tabbed Browsing has been added. Rather than only being able to look at one Web page at a time, or having to open another browser window to look at another Web page, you can open many tabs at the same time, in one browser window. This makes it easy to go back and forth between different Web pages with a single mouse click.

In addition, when you save multiple tabs to your favorites list, all the tabs are saved at the same time. This makes it really easy to go back to all of these pages with very few mouse clicks.

With your browser open, look under the toolbar. You will see two tabs. The first one is for the current page. Click on the untitled one and you will be given a blank browser window. Now you can navigate to another Web page on this new tab by typing its address.

What Is The Zoom Function?

In the lower right hand corner of your browser window is a magnifying glass with a percentage number. This is your zoom control for the entire Web page. You can zoom in or out and everything will get bigger, or smaller: images, text and background.

Text Size, which can be found under the page button on the toolbar, only changes the text size on a Web page. Use this if the default text size does not suit your viewing pleasure, but everything else looks okay.

What Is A Newsgroup?

A newsgroup is an online discussion or forum group, dealing with a wide range of topics. It is an electronic bulletin board of messages. People from all over the world can respond to other peoples' messages. You can even start new discussions.

Each newsgroup is focused on a particular topic. Usenet consists of over 25,000 newsgroups.

To access and review newsgroup postings, you need a newsreader. This ability is included in Windows Mail. Then you need to subscribe to the newsgroup so that the messages are downloaded automatically into your inbox.

Newsgroup messages are never private. Make sure you do not say anything that you wouldn't mind seeing on the front page of your newspaper the next day!

What Are Chat Rooms?

Chat rooms are the equivalent of meeting rooms in which you can carry on live keyboard conversations with everyone in the room as a group or with particular individuals.

There are two basic kinds of chats: Web-based and IRC (Internet Relay Channel). Web-based chat rooms are easier to access and are devoted to general subject matter.

Do you remember your mother telling you not to talk to strangers? Well, unless you already know the people in a chat room, they are all strangers. Be careful. Never, ever reveal any financial or personal information such as social security number or passport number in a chat room.

And once again, never say anything you wouldn't want to read about in tomorrow's newspaper.

What Is A Plug-In?

A plug-in is an auxiliary program that works alongside your browser. It is a script, utility, or a set of instructions that add to the functionality of a program without changing the program's base code. You download it, install it, and your browser will call on it only when it needs it.

Two great plug-ins are RealPlayer and Flash. RealPlayer is for Internet music and video broadcasts and Flash is for multimedia effects.

The best news is that if you need a plug-in to see or hear something, and you do not have it, you will automatically be offered a way to get it. Computers these days know when they need something and let you know, too.

What Is A Cookie?

A cookie is information from a Web site sent to a browser and stored on your hard drive so the Web site can retrieve it later. It is like an ID card. The next time you drop by the site, it will actually know your individual browser.

Most Web sites routinely log your visit. The cookie contains information that is recorded against your IP (Internet Protocol) address.

You have the option to configure your browser to accept or reject cookies. Open your browser, click on Tools, then Internet Options, then Privacy. By sliding the adjusting bar up and down, you can control how tough a cookie policy you want.

Some sites require your computer to accept cookies. If you need to go to that site, you have to accept their cookies.

What Is A Virus And Can I Protect My Computer?

A virus is an unwanted file or set of instructions that attaches itself to files in your computer system, usually causing harm to your computer. It replicates itself as the file is shared from computer to computer.

Viruses are not naturally occurring bugs. People who want to damage your computer system create them.

You can protect yourself from viruses by always checking programs and files that you download from the Internet, with a virus protection program. Most computers ship with a trial anti-virus program installed.

You can purchase protection programs from a computer store, direct from the software manufacturer and you can download them from the Internet. Some popular protection programs are McAfee's Anti Virus, Symantec's Norton Anti-Virus, Trend Micro PC-Cillian.

There is even a free program called AVG Free.

What Is A Virus And Can I Protect My Computer?, Cont.

Which is the best program to use? The best one is the one you will use. Get one. Update it frequently and use it all the time.

Even people you know and trust can accidentally send you a virus, so you really should use your virus protection all the time.

If your anti-virus program has an automatic e-mail protection system, use it.

For really robust protection of your computer, you should always use a Firewall, Anti-Virus program, Anti-Spyware Program, Anti-Ad Program and do not trust anything that comes in over the Internet, especially from any of your relatives!

How Do I Print A Web Page?

Printing a page from the Internet is easy. When you find something you like, click the Printer button on the toolbar, then Print or Print Preview.

One thing to keep in mind, Web pages were designed to be displayed on a monitor, not necessarily printed. What looks good on your computer might print horribly. If you see an option on a Web page for a Printer Friendly version, that will be your best bet to print. For example, a bank statement printed from the Web looks much better if they offer a printer friendly version.

If you want to print the page later, but you do not want to go back to the Web site, click the Page button on the toolbar, then Save As, give it a title and save it to your computer. You can come back to it at a later time and print it when it is convenient.

How Do I Log Off The Internet?

To log off, exit your browser by:

- Clicking the Close button on your browser

Or

- Look for a Sign Off command or Disconnect button.

If you are using a telephone dial-up modem, you may need to terminate the call manually, depending on how your program is set up.

If you are using a public computer, don't forget to clear your browsing history before you close the browser.

PART 11

E-Mail and Vista

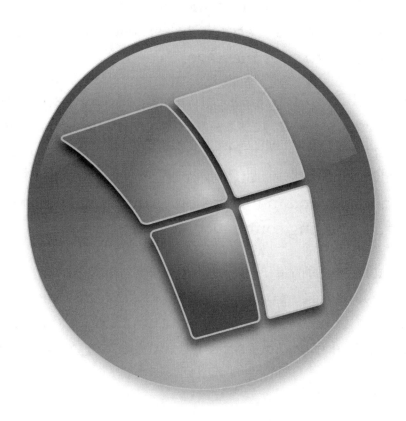

What Is E-Mail And How Does It Work?

E-mail is short for electronic mail. It is digital correspondence.

E-mail gives you the ability to send and receive text messages to or from anyone with an e-mail address. You can attach other files, pictures, or programs to your message.

E-mail is more like a conversation than a formal correspondence. It is a speedy way to get a message to someone. It should be concise, to the point and well written. Do not forget to check your spelling, grammar and punctuation. Your teachers were right. Spelling counts!

When someone sends you a message, that message is sent to your Internet Service Provider, and stored there. When you log on and check your e-mail, the message is sent from the server to your computer.

What Do I Need To Get Started?

- You need to be able to go online.
- You have to connect your modem to a telephone line, DSL line, cable TV or satellite dish.
- You must have an account with an Internet Service Provider.
- You will also need an e-mail software program (usually provided by your ISP) or use your browser for Webmail. One of the most popular e-mail programs is Microsoft's Windows Mail (Outlook Express in earlier operating versions of Windows). It is included with your Vista program so you do not have to use anything else.
- You have to have an e-mail address. You automatically get an e-mail address when you sign up with an ISP or online service.

Setting up is simple. The exact steps you follow to send and receive mail will vary from program to program. However, the e-mail options are always prominently displayed on the Menu screen and in their own drop-down menu.

What Do I Need To Get Started?, Cont.

Windows Mail is a great way to start your e-mail life. To create an e-mail account in Windows Mail, click on:

- Start.
- Type Windows Mail in the Search box.
- Click Windows Mail in the Start box.
- Click Tools.
- Click Accounts.
- Click Add.

You will need information from your ISP to set up Windows Mail: POP, SMTP, Login name and password. Answer a few more questions and you should be good to go.

Most ISPs have detailed instructions in the support section of their web site if you cannot make it work.

What Is In An E-Mail Address?

The Internet Service Provider assigns an e-mail address to you. Usually you can choose your user name.

The first part of the address, before the @ symbol, is a user name. The second part, or domain name, defines the Internet Service Provider, or business name, where the mail is sent. The two parts are separated by the @ sign (pronounced "at").

The domain name is followed by an extension that indicates the type of organization to which the network belongs.

Here is an example of an address:

Rebecca@theseniorsguide.com

How Do I Send E-Mail?

To send mail:

- Start your e-mail program.
- Click the Create New Mail (depending on your e-mail program, the name of this button may vary).
- Assign a Recipient in the To: box.
- Type a short description of the message in the subject line.
- Type your message.
- Check your spelling and grammar.
- Click Send.

Many people compose a number of e-mails prior to clicking send. This saves connection time if you use a dialup connection.

How Can I Be Sure That A Message Was Sent?

If you are not sure if you really sent a message, there is a way to find out.

Look through your icons or menu choices for the Out Box. With Windows Mail or Outlook (Outlook is a full-featured productivity tool in the Microsoft Office product line), if the mail has been sent, the out box is empty. Other mail programs may have some indication that the mail has been sent, such as the message is marked with a check mark.

The Outbox is Empty

With Windows Mail or Outlook, a Sent Message file is in your filing cabinet that you can check. Windows Mail and Outlook take messages from the Out Box, sends them, and files a copy in the Sent Message file. You can control how this is done through the Tools tab in either program.

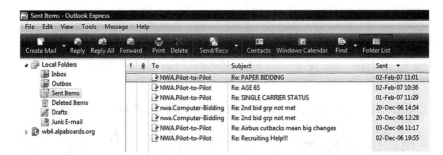

If Your E-mail is Listed in the Sent Items Folder, It Really Was Sent

How Do I Receive And Read E-Mail?

To check for new mail you need to be in your e-mail program and be online.

- Click Send and Receive, or Check for New Messages. When new mail arrives, depending on the program, you may hear a sound, get a message and/or see a little envelope in your system tray. Of course you can always look in the Inbox.
- To read a message, if there is a preview pane, just scroll through it. If you double click the message header, it will open in a single viewer.

As with sending mail, most folks read their mail offline.

Once the e-mail is read, you can reply to the sender, reply to everyone listed as a recipient, forward to someone else, save it, print it or throw it out.

How Do I Use the Contacts List In Windows Mail?

Contacts, or what many people might call an address book, is where you will keep information about people you want to communicate with. Not only can you store their e-mail address here, but their snail mail address, phone numbers, Web pages and any other information you might want to apply to them.

When you are in the Contacts list, highlight an entry and then select e-mail from the toolbar if you want to send them an e-mail.

From a message, click the To: box and the Contact list will pop up. Select who you want to send the e-mail to and then click OK. You will be back to your new mail message with the recipient's name in the To: box.

Vista coordinates the contacts list for use with a number of programs.

How Do I Reply To E-Mail?

To reply to an e-mail message:

- Click on a message header to open it.
- Click on the Reply button. This will automatically copy the original message and address it back to the sender, if you have set up your preferences that way. (This is a good idea so that whatever you write can be referenced to the original message.)
- Type your message.
- Click the Send button.

The Reply All button will send a copy of your reply to everyone in the To:, CC: and Bcc: lists. Try not to use Reply All unless everyone on the list really needs to see your message.

For example, if your sibling sends you a joke via e-mail, you might be one of a hundred on the distribution list. All one hundred do not need to know that you laughed when you read it.

How Do I Forward E-Mail?

To forward e-mail:

- Click the Forward button.
- In the To: Box, type the address of the person you are sending the message to.
- Add any additional text you want in the body of the message.
- Click the Send button.

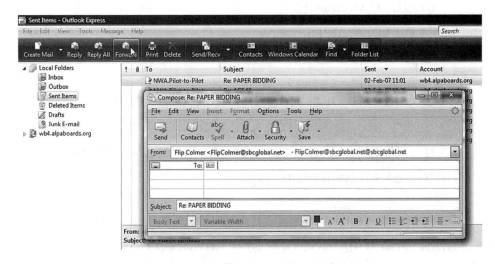

Forwarding an E-mail

How Do I Send Carbon Copies And Blind Carbon Copies?

If you want to send two or more people the same message, and you do not mind if they know who else is receiving it:

- Type one address in the To: box (or as many people as you want).
- Type the other address in the CC (carbon copy) field (once again, as many as you want).

To send a mailing without disclosing the list of recipients, put yourself in the To: Box, and everyone else in BCC (blind carbon copy) field (once again, as many as you want).

If you put recipients into the BCC field, their names and addresses are masked from all others. However, anyone, including those in BCC can see who is in the To: and CC: fields.

How Do I Attach A File To My E-Mail Message?

To send a file, such as a word processing document, spreadsheet, or a photo:

- In the mail menu, click Attach File or Send Attachments. Or, click on the "paper clip" icon on the toolbar.
- You will be prompted for the file name and its location on your hard drive. Browse to the file.
- Double-click on it. A copy of it will be attached to your e-mail. Click send when you have finished this piece of mail.

Keep in mind that viruses can be hidden in attachments. Some people, as a safeguard, never open attachments, even from people they know and trust. If the file is small enough, it is better to insert the text or photos into the body of your e-mail.

How Do I Receive Attachments?

When someone sends you an e-mail with an attachment, you will generally see it as an icon at the bottom of your e-mail, with a name next to it. In most cases, you can just double-click on the icon.

Do not open an attachment if you do not know who sent it to you. Some attachments can contain viruses that can harm your entire computer.

Even if you do know who sent it to you, be very careful about opening attachments. As mentioned on the previous page, viruses lurk in attachments. You can save the attachment without opening it, scan it with anti-virus software and if it is deemed safe, then you can open it.

What Is Web Mail?

Web mail is e-mail that you look at with a Web browser, rather than your e-mail program. Not every ISP supports this. Check with your provider to see if they do.

The benefit of this is that you do not need to have your computer with you if you are on the road and need to check your e-mail. You simply surf to the ISP's Web Mail Web site using any computer, type in your user name and password, and now you are looking at your e-mail that is on the ISP's server. You can read the mail, answer it, forward it and delete it. If you delete the mail, it is removed from the server.

However, if you leave it there, it will stay there until you download it into your e-mail program, next time you ask for your mail at home.

What Is POP Mail And How Do I Use It?

POP stands for Post Office Protocol. It's what allows different e-mail programs to work together around the Internet. So long as your ISP supports POP mail, you can use whatever e-mail client you want to.

To set up a POP mail account, you will need some ISP information: POP and SMTP settings, login name and password. Your ISP's Web site probably has a page dedicated to setting up a POP mail account. Once you have this information, open your POP enabled e-mail program, such as Windows Mail. Then click:

- Tools.
- Accounts.
- New.
- E-mail.

Follow the on-screen instructions and fill in the information as needed. The last step tests the connection and settings.

Do I Need To Use E-Mail Security?

E-mail is how viruses get spread throughout the Internet. It is a best practice to have an anti-virus program that not only scans incoming e-mail, but scans your outgoing e-mail as well.

If you have a choice of ISPs, choose one that has an anti-virus protocol at the server level.

Make sure your firewall is turned on.

Don't open attachments unless they are scanned for viruses.

Is E-Mail Private?

No. E-mail is never confidential. Without encryption, the possibility exists that e-mail can be accessed and read by others.

Your recipient can forward it to others. Once it is out of your computer, the whole world could see it.

Do not send anything that you would not mind reading about on the front page of your local newspaper. The next day! It's amazing how fast things spread via the Internet.

What Is Spam And How Do I Block It?

Although Spam is my husband's favorite luncheon meat, spam means unwanted e-mail coming to your e-mail address. This comes from Internet marketers trying to sell you stuff, con artists trying to steal your stuff and smart alecks trying to play with your stuff.

Never, ever respond to a spam e-mail. Even if it has a link that says "remove me from your mailing list." Sometimes this is a way to see whether or not this is a valid and active recipient. You may receive even more spam if you try to get off their lists.

Never, ever click a link on a spam message. It might activate a virus. It might take you to a Web site designed to steal your identity. Even if the e-mail says it comes from a trusted site, such as a store you know, it's best to manually type the real address into the address bar and then go to it.

Never, ever buy something from an e-mail solicitation. Once again, it is best to check out the company by manually typing in the address, checking with the Better Business Bureau, or checking with a number of online business reviewers. And once again, if you decide to purchase, do not use the e-mail link to get there.

What Is Spam And How Do I Block It?, Cont.

A recent spam looked just like my bank's e-mail stationary. Most trusted institutions will never send an e-mail asking for personal information, account numbers or passwords. This one did. I called my bank and they confirmed that this spam was going around. Although I make it sound as if there is only bad out there, if you use these precautions I outlined, you should be able to protect yourself.

Spam filters are used to sort out the bad e-mails from the good and move them into your Deleted Items or Junk Mail folder. You can train your spam filter to know what is good and what is not. Also, some ISPs have spam filters at the server level for added protection. Use them as you would an antivirus program: all the time.

Spam filters can make mistakes so you should check the spam or junk folder for real mail before you empty it, just in case.

In your preferences section, turn off Read Receipt. This normally sends out a message to a sender that you have read the e-mail. This is another way Junk Mail senders find out that your e-mail address is active.

What Is Spam And How Do I Block It?, Cont.

Most ISPs give you multiple e-mail boxes. You can create a second e-mail address that you use for everyone outside of your family and friends. That way you can protect your personal e-mail account by not giving it to businesses, strangers who want to communicate with you or anyone else not in your "circle of trust."

How Do I Send A Web Page?

If you find a Web page that you want someone else to see, you have two options. You can send them the page itself, or you can send them a link to the Web page. You do this by clicking:

- Page on the toolbar, then the option you want.
- Your e-mail pane will open. Put the address into the To: box of the person you want to send the page or link to. Add a subject line and a note.
- Click Send.

Your message is now in the Outbox of your e-mail program. The next time you click send in your e-mail program, the Web page will go out.

What Are Emoticons?

Emoticons, or Smileys are keyboard created characters that may appear somewhere in an e-mail to reinforce what was just said or to add some personality to the message. They are created by combining different punctuation keystrokes, with letters and numbers, to make a picture. Here are a few as examples:

Emoticon	What It Means
:-) or :) or ☺	Smiling, Happy
:-}	Grinning
:-D	Laughing
:-1	Smirking
:-(or ☹	Frowning, Sad
:-\ or ☺	Undecided

Turn your head sideways if this just looks like punctuation.

One last one is (g) or (G). This stands for grinning, or grinning really big. Use this to let someone know that you are joking or smiling when you typed something.

Is There E-Mail Etiquette?

While online, you should always practice good social skills and behavior. Since you will often be communicating with people that you do not know, or cannot tell what your mood is at the moment, you should always follow some basic rules.

No SHOUTING. Typing in all upper case signifies shouting. You can use upper case for emphasis in a word or two. ANY MORE THAN THAT AND YOU'RE SHOUTING.

No flaming. When another online person posts an opinion that you think is outrageous or ridiculous, do not be tempted to respond with excessive outrage. Keep your temper and language under control.

No spamming. Do not post the same message to hundreds of newsgroups. Do not forward mail in bulk to everyone in your contacts list.

Save your humor and jokes for good friends and close confidants. Humor can easily be misinterpreted. One person's joke is another person's spam.

What Are Acronyms And What Are They Used For?

Acronyms are short hand expressions that are used in e-mails, chat sessions and text messaging to save time. Here are some of the more widely used ones:

Acronym	What It Means
AFAIK	As far as I know.
BRB	Be right back.
BTW	By the way...
IMHO	In my humble opinion.
EOL	End of lecture.
TIA	Thanks in advance.
LOL	Laughing out loud.
GMTA	Great minds think alike.
TTFN	Ta ta for now.
WYSIWYG	What you see is what you get.
IANALB	I am not a lawyer, but...
FWIW	For what it's worth.
ROTFL	Rolling on the floor laughing.
IDK	I don't know.
TTYL	Talk to you later.

1. Windows Vista's Basic and Classic versions will interface with most graphics hardware that supports Windows XP.

2. When you run the Upgrade Advisor it will automatically update itself so that you get the latest changes.

3. Print or save the full report before exiting the Upgrade Advisor.

4. You can set Windows to accept a single-click instead of the default double-click.

5. If there are too many tasks to fit on the Taskbar, Windows will group like items together.

6. If you click the Help button in any folder, it will open the Help and Support Center positioned at a relevant topic.

7. Windows Vista's default power-off state is Sleep mode, which records the contents of memory to the hard disk (just like Hibernate) but also maintains the memory for a period of time (as in XP's Standby mode).

8. When you perform a search with Vista's new, instant search feature, you can save the search in a special folder. This powerful feature allows you to create a virtual folder which, by default, is saved in your \\ Searches\ folder. Every time you open such a folder, the search results are updated.

9. In Windows Vista, you can add additional clocks to the system tray. Click the clock, and then click Date and Time Settings. Click the Additional Clocks tab. You can add one or two additional clocks to the tray and select their time zones.

10. You can save your progress in most of the games included with Windows Vista — even the carry-overs from earlier versions of Windows.

11. You can create XML documents, which are more secure than regular text files or even word processor docs. Just create a document in a word processor, print it via the options menu, and select the XPS printer.

12. File names and folder names can be very long, but they can't contain the following characters: \ / : * ? " < >|

13. Files and folders on floppy drives, key drives, and network drives are really deleted when you delete them. The Recycle Bin doesn't work on floppies, key drives, or drives attached to other computers on your network.

14. Shadow copies are also called previous versions or back-up copies of your data files, which Vista keeps for you automatically. However, if you have Vista home or Vista Home Premium, you don't get shadow copies protection.

15. If you choose a CD or DVD drive for automatic back-ups, you need to remember to put a blank CD or DVD in the drive before the backup runs.

16. Windows Vista games deposit their saves into a special directory, called Saved Games, in your personal folder. In theory, that will make upgrading to a new system much easier for gamers, who like to migrate their game saves.

17. When using the Help system, it's usually advanta-geous to include Microsoft's online database in your search. The online/offline status of your search is lo-cated on the bottom right of the Help window. You can click it to toggle

18. The Games folder is a powerful repository of all things gaming. From within, you launch games, up-date games with the latest patches, enable parental controls to protect younger users from harmful con-tent, and more. Invoke it by clicking Start/Games.

19. Do you use the icon in the upper left corner of system and application windows? A quick double-click closes the window (instead of a single click on the X at the upper right). Though Microsoft left the icon out in Vista, the function remains.

20. In Microsoft Windows Explorer, you can use col-umn headers (Name, Size, and so on) to sort files. Savvy users may right-click on a column head to re-move items or add some — say, Dimensions for im-ages. There are around 45 such columns available in Windows XP. Windows Vista has well over 250, cover-ing a multitude of metadata.

21. The new Program Menu shows you only recently used applications and requires extra clicks to navigate to submenus. This can be very frustrating but, thank-fully, the Search box Microsoft has added to the Start menu is a great replacement. As quickly as you can type, it returns intelligent results in apps, files, even e-mail messages.

22. Unlike previous versions of Windows, Vista's Task Scheduler wakes up a PC that's suspended or hibernating, runs the scheduled task, and then puts the PC back to sleep.

23. Previous versions of Windows provided Outlook Express to support the e-mail functions. In Windows Vista, this is replaced by Windows Mail.

24. For e-mail, click the box to ask Windows Mail to remember the password, so you don't have to enter it each time you send or receive mail.

25. The windows Contacts folder replaces the Windows Address Book found in previous versions of Windows.

26. Marking a message as not junk will move that message to your Inbox, but future messages from that sender might still end up in the junk e-mail folder.

27. The Windows Security Center has an irritating habit of not properly identifying installed software.

28. You can remove an icon from the Windows desktop by right-clicking it and choosing Delete, or by clicking it once and pressing Delete.

29. Task Manager: Press Ctrl+Shift+Esc.

30. Tasks Screen: Press Ctrl+Alt+Del.

31. To launch the shortcuts on the Quick Launch toolbar: Press Windows logo key + 1-0.

32. To cycle through programs on Taskbar: Press Windows logo key + T.

33. To bring all gadgets to the front and select windows Sidebar: Press Windows logo key + Spacebar.

34. To cycle through Sidebar gadgets: Press Windows logo key + G.

35. To open Windows Mobility Center: Press Windows logo key + X.

36. To open a folder, press and release Alt to show the Menu Bar (also works in Internet Explorer).

37. You can speed up your PC on the fly by simply plugging in a USB drive (or iPod or Compact Flash card or any external drive) with some spare megabytes.

38. You can find the Command bar just below the Address bar and here you can start different activities, depending on the files that are contained in the folder you are currently in. Therefore, if you access a folder with images, you have the option to open the pictures with Windows Photo Gallery, send them through e-mail or Burn a pictures CD.

39. Navigation Pane: this pane contains two sections: Favorite links — that provides access to some of your favorite links like Documents and Pictures — and Folders, which displays the location you are currently browsing.

40. Details Pane: detailed information (Date Modified, Authis, Size) about a certain file or folder is displayed in the Details Pane. You can also add you own tags and your own categories, which can help you when searching for that specific file/folder.

41. Preview Pane is located on the right hand side and it allows you to view the content of a file without opening it.

42. Command Bar gives you the option to Organize your files and folders, change the View and even Print or Burn a file/folder on a CD/DVD. Address Bar displays the location you are currently in and you can also type a URL and have the Explorer display a Web page.

43. Search Box allows you to search files and folders on your computer.

44. Every anti-spyware application (free or paid) MUST have the following features: 1. Effective real time protection against all spyware-related threats that may attack your computer. 2. The backup and restore functions are vital necessities. 3. Automatic updates are a must, also. 4. Detailed scanning results and descriptions of encountered problems. 5. The ability to completely remove all files, directories and registry entries associated with a certain spyware threat. 6. Easy to install and use for every average computer user. 7. Scheduled scanning is another feature worth its weight in gold. 8. The ability to set scanning options manually, and also have access to quick and full scan modes.

45. Pressing F1 opens Help information in most programs.

46. To avoid problems, close all open programs before starting any program installation.

47. A zip drive is a type of disk with a higher density than a floppy disk. You can store more information on it than a floppy disk.

48. To rename a shortcut icon, simply right-click the icon, select Rename, and type in a new name. Press enter.

49. If you subscribe to an online mailing list, be sure you know how to unsubscribe.

50. When describing a CD or DVD, the term "disc" is used instead of "disk." They are pronounced the same.

51. Changing the magnification on your screen only changes the way text appears. Zooming in (and out) doesn't physically alter the text itself.

52. Undo command: Ctrl + Z.

53. Redo command: Ctrl + Y.

54. Cut: Ctrl + X, Copy: Ctrl + C, Paste: Ctrl + V.

55. Save a file: Ctrl + S.

56. Check your spelling: F7.

57. If you don't want any home page — allowing your browser to appear on the screen faster — click the down arrow next to the Home icon, choose Remove, and click the home page.

58. As you hover over a drive or folder in the Folders list, it expands to reveal the subfolders.

59. The Cut command removes the selection. It turns gray until you Paste it. If you change your mind, put the cursor back and select Paste.

60. Files and folders that you delete from the Command Prompt, don't go into the Recycle Bin. Also, there's no recycle bin for drives with removable media.

61. Right-click the Recycle Bin icon and select Empty Recycle Bin, to remove all of the files and folders without it being open.

62. Compressed folders are distinguished from other folders by a zipper on the folder icon.

63. To create a compressed folder and copy a file into it at the same time: right-click a file, select Send To, Compressed (zipped) Folder. The new compressed folder has the same file name, but a file extension of .zip.

64. When you install new programs, their entries automatically appear under All Programs, positioned alphabetically, or in a new folder within All Programs.

65. Not all the Start menu features and functions apply when you use the Classic Start menu.

66. Press Alt + Enter to make the Command Prompt window full screen if it's windowed, or vice versa.

67. Mistyping a URL can display sites that take advantage of common typing errors to parody genuine Web sites, so be very careful.

68. You don't have to type the http:// prefix, since Internet Explorer will assume this and provide it automatically.

69. You can right-click any link in a web page or in search results, and select Add to Favorites.

70. Web mail stores and retains your e-mail on a mail server. The main Web mail services are particularly subject to spam messages, although the service provider will usually detect and transfer such messages into a separate folder.

71. If you click and drag a file into the Photo Gallery window, the file gets copied to your Pictures folder — even if it isn't a picture file.

72. If you delete a photo from the Photo Gallery, Vista deletes the file — so the picture not only disappears from the Gallery, but it also disappears period. You can get it out of the Recycle Bin if it wasn't on a network drive.

73. Tags that you assign to a picture travel with the picture.

74. Make it a priority to download new versions of your browser when they are released.

75. When using a search function, a keyword is the word the user wants to find in a document.

76. Software piracy is the unauthorized copying of software.

77. Pixels are clusters of colored dots that combine to form images on the computer screen.

78. Cache is a small amount of computer memory that holds most recently used data.

79. Do not delete program files. If you want to get rid of a program, uninstall it.

80. Do not use the lower case L for the number one, or a capital O for zero. The computer is literal and treats them very differently.

81. To scroll continuously, hold the mouse button down instead of just clicking.

82. If you seem to be typing over text instead of inserting new text, you may have depressed the INSERT key. To deactivate INSERT, simply press it again.

83. In printing, the direction of the paper is called orientation. Portrait means that the paper is taller than it is wide. Landscape means the paper is wider than it is tall.

84. A newsgroup is often called a forum. It is an online discussion group where people exchange ideas about a common interest.

85. Malware (malicious software) is designed to deliberately harm your computer. To protect your system, you need up-to-date antivirus and anti-spyware software. Only the latter is provided as part of Windows, so you'll need a separate antivirus program.

86. Firewall is on by default in Windows Vista, but you can turn it off if you have another Firewall installed and active.

87. System Restore is not intended for personal data files.

88. The ability to set up automatic backups is not included in Windows Vista Starter and Windows Vista Home Basic editions.

89. To play DVDs you must have a DVD drive and a compatible DVD decoder, such as provided on systems that include Windows Media Center.

90. Some windows are fixed and cannot be resized. These include dialog boxes and applications, such as Windows calculator.

91. Unless you specifically tell Windows Mail that you want it to download and show you pictures inside e-mail messages, it won't.

92. To cancel a document from printing, select that document. In the print queue window, choose Document, Cancel. Or, right-click the document in the print queue window and choose Cancel.

93. Copying from a CD is also known as ripping.

94. To add gadgets to the sidebar: Click the + at the top of the side bar. Drag the icon of the gadget you want to your side bar and the gadget will appear!

95. Ever wanted to talk to your computer? Click the Start Orb. Click Control Panel. Click Speech Recognition. Click Start Speech Recognition.

96. Leave your computer on for as long as you can. I leave my computer on for months on end. Every time I restart my computer, the cache to certain folders, files, etc. is deleted.

97. The Windows Firewall now has the option to configure incoming and outgoing traffic, which I think is great. It comes in very handy when you need it most.

98. Keep files organized. I keep all my pictures, videos, documents... everything is organized. I truly think it is very helpful to know where all your files and folders are. This way, they are also not thrown all over the place so you forget what you're looking for.

99. Delete software that you do not need from "Remove Programs."

100. Running Programs. Always check what programs/ processes you have running on your computer through the task manager. It usually helps because some programs will stop responding in the background if you have one that is taking up a huge amount of resources. You might experience some lag.

101. Go have some fun! Happy Computing!
Visit www.theseniorsguide.com and her sister site: www.MeAndMyCaregivers.com.

101 Terrific Web Sites

1. The Senior's Guide Series
   www.theseniorsguide.com

2. MeAndMyCaregiver(s), Inc.
   www.MeAndMyCaregivers.com

3. Graphic Design
   www.cricketbow.com

4. American Factfinder
   http://factfinder.census.gov/home/

5. One Look Online Dictionary
   www.onelook.com

6. MapQuest
   www.mapquest.com

7. NoNags
   www.nonags.com

8. Bored
   www.bored.com

9. The bunk stops here!
   www.purportal.com

10. USPS Zipcode+4 Lookup
    http://zip4.usps.com/zip4

11. U.S. Government's Official Web Site
    www.usa.gov

12. Get your mail from POP3 Accounts
    www.mail2web.com

13. Online Almanac
    www.infoplease.com

14. Internet Movie Database
    http://imdb.com

15. Internet Public Library
    www.ipl.org
16. Price Watch
    www.pricewatch.com
17. How Things Work
    www.howstuffworks.com
18. World History
    www.hyperhistory.com
19. Fodor's Restaurant Guide
    www.fodors.com/world/restaurant finder.html
20. Virtual Reference Desk
    www.itools.com
21. The Why Files
    www.whyfiles.org
22. Genealogy
    www.cyndislist.com
23. Golf Courses
    www.golfcourse.com
24. Web Solutions
    www.R3WebSolutions.com
25. American Association of Retired Persons
    www.aarp.org
26. Baby Boomer's Headquarters
    www.bbhq.com
27. Habitat for Humanity
    www.habitat.org
28. Jewish Information Center
    www.jewishnet.net

29. Romeo Computers
    www.romeocomp.com
30. WW2 MIA
    www.bentprop.org
31. Astrology
    www.astrologyzone. com
32. Reiki Healing
    www.samarasays.com
33. The Smithsonian Institute
    www.si.edu
34. American Museum of Natural History
    www.amnh.org
35. The Kentucky Horse Park
    www.imh.org
36. The National Corvette Museum
    www.corvettemuseum.com
37. San Diego Aerospace Museum
    www.AerospaceMuseum.org
38. Veterans News and Information Source
    www.vnis.com
39. AAA Online
    www.aaa.com
40. U.S. Postal Service
    www.usps.gov
41. Britannica Online
    www.eb.com
42. Interesting Videos
    www.youtube.com

43. Kelly Blue Book
    www.kbb.com

44. Social Security Online
    www.ssa.gov

45. Kiplinger Online
    www.kiplinger.com

46. Investment FAQs
    www.invest-faq.com

47. NASDAQ
    www.nasdaq.com

48. Cancer Nutrition Info
    www.cancernutritioninfo.com

49. Digital Photography
    www.fickr.com

50. Fashion
    www.zoomzoom.com

51. Food 411
    www.food411.com

52. Home Improvement
    www.digitalhome.cnet.com

53. The Living to 100 Life Expectancy Calculator
    www.livingto100.com.

54. Pets
    www.dogster.com

55. Social Networking
    www.ineighbors.org

56. Travel Bookings
    www.sidestep.com

57. Classifieds
    www.craigslist.org

58. Comparison Shopping
    www.shopzilla.com.

59. Deal of the Day
    www.woot.com

60. Kitsch
    www.mcphee.com

61. Shoes
    www.zappos.com

62. When Things Go Wrong
    www.complaints.com

63. TV News
    www.blinkxtv.com

64. Consumer Protection
    www.idtheftcenter.org.

65. General Reference
    www.answers.com

66. Legal Matters
    www.findlaw.com

67. Politics
    www.publicagenda.org

68. Web Search
    www.clusty.com.

69. Animation
    www.aardman.com

70. Books
    www.complete-review.com

71. Classical Music
    opus1classical.com
72. Galleries
    www.coudal.com/moom.php
73. Games
    www.orisinal.com
74. Humor
    www.mcsweeneys.net
75. More Funny Stuff
    www.zefrank.com
76. Podcasting
    www.podcastbunker.com.
77. Radio
    www.mercora.com
78. Television
    www.tv.com
79. Forbes
    www.forbes.com
80. Elder Law Answers
    www.McDermott.elderlawanswers.com
81. Bingo
    www.bingozone.com
82. Friend Finder
    www.meetasenior.com
83. Medical Info
    www.webmd.com
84. Welcome to the White House
    www.whitehouse.gov

85. National Hospice Organization
    www.nho.org
86. American Cancer Society
    www.cancer.org
87. Ask the Dietician
    www.dietician.com
88. Administration on Aging
    www.aoa.gov
89. Wine
    www.wine.com
90. Classic Cars
    www.classiccar.com
91. Recipes
    www.epicurious.com
92. American Kennel Club
    www.aka.org
93. National Public Radio
    www.npr.org
94. NASCAR
    www.nascar.com
95. Movies
    www.movies.com
96. Hotels
    www.hotels.com
97. Ice cream
    www.benjerrys.com
98. Sleep
    www.sleepnet.com

99. American Contract Bridge
    www.acbl.org

100. Weather
     www.weather.com

101. Computer Help
     www.theseniorsguide.com

Index

Index

Index

Notes

The Senior's Guide to the Internet